The Romani Collection

RROMANE PARAMICHA

SERIES EDITOR: AGGOTT HÖNSCH ISTVÁN

RROMANE PARAMICHA
STORIES AND LEGENDS OF THE GURBETI ROMA

HEDINA TAHIROVIĆ SIJERČIĆ

MAGORIA BOOKS

2009

Rromane Paramicha by Hedina Tahirović Sijerčić

Illustrated by Doris Greven

© Copyright 2009 Hedina Tahirović Sijerčić

Edited by Noelle Pirie

Cover design by Sebestyén, using illustration by Doris Greven.

First Edition

ISBN 978-0-9811626-2-1

Published by MAGORIA BOOKS

www.MagoriaBooks.com

LIBRARY AND ARCHIVES CANADA CATALOGUING IN PUBLICATION

Tahirović Sijerčić, Hedina, 1960-
Rromane paramicha = stories and legends of the Gurbeti Roma /
by Hedina Tahirović Sijerčić.

(The Romani collection) ISBN 978-0-9811626-2-1
1. Romanies–Former Yugoslav republics–Folklore. 2. Tales–Former
Yugoslav republics. 3. Legends–Former Yugoslav republics.
4. Romani language–Dialects–Texts. I. Title. II. Title: Stories and
legends of the Gurbeti Roma. III. Series: Romani collection

DX157.T34 2009   398.2089'91497   C2009-903007-1

Istardipe · Contents

Ilustracija: Doris Greven
Recenzija: Ronald Lee
Lektorka pe Rromani chib: Elvira Rašiti
Lektoro pe Englecki chib: Ronald Lee

Swaturai Mai Angle

Katar o Ronald Lee
Instruktori Semestralno
E Romani Diaspora Ande Kanada
NEW343H1S
Universitato Torontosko
Toronto

Shavále, Rromale! Ande'l purané gesá, amé, le Rromá samas bi-sikadé. Chi mai ramosardyás chi yek Rrom worka Rromní amare paramichia tai hiria. Numa kana avilé le Komunisti ande Ivropa pala o Duito Marimos, but Rroma sikádyile ande wushkála. Le terné shavé musai sas lenga te zhan ande wushkála. Kakale Rromá sikadé ramosardé bukfi, kerdiné gazeti tai kerdiné programuria po radio tai po tele-vizhono. Amari pen, E Hedina Sijercic, Bosniaki Rromní katar o Sarayevo, si Rromní sikadí kai kerelas bukí sar jurnal-ista, wuchitelka tai produktorka kai kerdyas programuria pe'l Rromende ando Sarayevo, o mai baró foró ande Bosnia kai woi beshelas mai anglal te avel ande Kanada peske familiása. Laki vica si Gurberi ande Bosnia. Kana woi sas ande Bosnia, woi ramosardyas but paramichiya kai zhanelas le Rromá ande Bosnia, le Chergaria tai le Rrom Xoraxané, le Rrom kerenge kai beshen ande'l fori ando lako tem.

Ages, amáre terné Rromá bishtrén kakalé paramichia ande'l temá. Zhan le shavoré ande wushkála, beshen anglal o televízhono sor o ges tai hamin-pe desyá but le terné Gazhensa. Ande Kanada, amare Rrom purané zhanenas but paramichia numa agés – kon zhanél kakalé paramichia? Sa bilaile sar o iv.

Kakalé paramichia si amari Rromani kultura tai musai

te ramos len te na bishtérdion. Amare terné Rromá musai te zhanén penge historia tai pengi kultura. Amari pen, e Hedina, azhutil sa le Rrom ande sa'l temá kana ramol kakalé paramichia. Akana, amare terné shavé shai sikion kakale paramichia te na bishtérdion..

Te del o Del baxt, sastimus la Hedinake, amari Rromani pen.

Introduction

By Ronald Lee
Sessional Instructor
The Romani Diaspora
NEW343H1S
New College
University of Toronto

Until the 20th century, the Romani culture and traditions were transmitted orally and while outsiders sometimes recorded folktales and legends from various Romani story tellers, the Roma themselves were not a literate people and were not able to record their culture for posterity. In the 20th century, especially in the former Communist countries of eastern Europe, large numbers of Roma were educated and some began to record their music, poetry and folktales. Hedina Sijercic is one of these educated Roma who formerly worked as a radio and TV journalist in Sarajevo, Bosnia and later on as a teacher and journalist in Toronto / Canada. During this time she recorded numerous folktales and legends from her own family and other Roma, stories that had been told around the campfires of nomadic Chergari Roma and in the "mahali" or settlements of the sedentary Gurbeti Roma.

These stories are now gradually being forgotten by the Roma in most countries because of assimilation, television and other factors which are bringing the young Roma more and more into contact with the non-Romani societies around them. In Canada, my generation was the last to be able to tell these stories in Romani and today, the art of telling folktales in Romani survives mainly among the more isolated and nomadic groups.

These folktales, however, are part of the Romani culture and are worthy of preservation. Among the Roma in different countries and among differing clans, the same themes often appear. For instance, Hedina's story about "O Dilo, or The Fool", has its parallels in "Kalderash" or nomadic Copper-smith legends as "O Dilo Yanko" (Foolish Yanko) and even in Welsh Romani tales as "O Dilino Jak" (Foolish Jack). They are, of course, related to the Jack-and-the-beanstalk genre of folktales in English folklore, the theme of the silly younger brother who turns out not to be so silly after all. How God Made the Roma is also widely known by Roma in many differing versions. The Legend of the Nail also has many variants among different groups of Roma. In the Middle Ages, rumours spread that the Roma had made the nails with which Christ had been crucified. The Roma then created a counter legend in which a Roma or a Romani stole one of the nails and was then blessed by Jesus who said that He would protect the Roma because of this kindness.

This collection of tales recorded by Hedina can be con-sidered to be a valuable addition to Romani folklore. None have been published, at least in English, except in our own "Romano Lil", the first Canadian Romani quarterly publica-tion, and most are original to the Bosnian Roma. The fact that the tales are also written in Romani as well as in their English translations is also a plus since this will enable both the Roma themselves and those who wish to study a living Romani dialect to learn the stories in Romani.

I would therefore recommend this collection of Romani folk tales as a valuable contribution to the presentation of our culture to Canadians in general and commend the author for her dedication to our current program of Public Education and Awareness which is designed to combat the 'Gypsy' stereotype by presenting the true history and culture of the Roma to the outside world.

Pala mrne chavore Edis thaj Zerin

To my sons Edis and Zerin

Rachako

Ka thovav e jagali memelin
pasha e kunate.
Ka thovav e parni purum
pe chavoreske chuchorate.

Ka thovav e shulavdi
pala udaresko
Ka rudjavav e rudjipe Devlesko.

Te nashalav e chavoresko rovipe,
Te nashalav las,
E choxana.

At Night

I am going to leave the lamp on
next to the cradle.
I am going to rub a garlic clove
over the child's breast.

I am going to put the broom
behind the door.
I am going to pray to God.

To drive away the child's crying,
To drive away the bloodsucking butterfly,
The vampire moth - a *choxana*.

Dukhadi Madjija - Jakhalipe

E dzungalenge jakha dikhen tut
Sar o paj mudaren tut!
Nasvalipe-nash tutar!
Andare chire shorestar
Andare chire kolinestar
Andare chire vastendar
Andare chire porestar
Andare chire prnalendar
Nash tutar,
Ando dzungale jakha!

Duj jakha
Duj vasta
Duj prnala
E jakhesko dukh
Dza ando prnalende
Dza andare prnalendar
Ande phuvjate.

Dza andare phuvjatar
Ando mulipeste!
Nash!

Magic Spell against Pain

Evils eyes are looking at you
Like rampaging water
They will destroy you.
Illness! - Begone
From your head
From your chest
From your hands
From your stomach
From your legs
Begone!
Back into the evil eyes!

Two eyes
Two hands
Two legs
Pain in the eyes
Go away into the legs
Go away from the legs
Into the earth.

Go away from the earth
Into death.
Go away!

Sovimahchi Djiljori

Chutem kuna tala e pruna,
Si ma chavo te dav kuna,
Brshind del thaj najarel leh,
Patra peren, ucharen leh,
Buzni nakhel, chuchi del leh,
Bahval phurdel, sovljarel leh.

Purani djili

Lullaby

I will put a cradle under a plum tree,
I will lull my child to sleep;
When it rains, the rain will bathe him,
When the leaves fall, they will hide him,
When a goat passes, it will feed him,
When the wind blows, it will calm him.

Traditional

Jekh Bendjali Familija

Lungo vakto nakhada sar pe themeste naj seha manushen, thaj kana o Del thaj e Phuv dzivina ando baxtaripeste. Von seha-len pandz chavore. Angluno sasa o Thagar Kham, dujto o Thagar Chon, trito e Thagarica Jag, shtarto o Thagar Balval, thaj pandzto sasa e Thagarica Turnjiko Parnimata. Lenge chavore avile ando sajekhesko chingareste dziko bajrovipeste. O Del thaj e Phuv cherde dushmajeske situacije mashkaro peske, thaj thode pire chavore ande armajeste. Odolese, murshikane chavore avile ratvale thaj cherde jekh plano sar te chingaren lenge phure.

Plano sasa te uladiven len. Thoska uladipesko, sako shaj te dza opashin e themeste te cheren piro cher.

O Thagar Kham vacharda:"Me dzav te tatarav pe Phuvjate e saste zuralipesa. I dej Phuv na kamel baro tatipe, thaj ako tu, mo phral Chon, na ikloves, voj shaj te phabarel. Gova plano shaj te uladivel i dej thaj o dad."

O Thagar Chon phenda: "Ando vakto kana tu tatares pe dejate, me dzav te akharav sa chehrajine. Chehrajine dzan te chelen chelipe pasha o dad, thaj te idjaren les dur e dejatar."

Akana o Thagar Balval vacharda: "Me sem tumenca. Me dzav te phurdav pe dejate e saste zuralipesa dziko o dad uladivel latar."

Angluno, o Thagar Kham astarda te chingarel. Vov tatarda pe dejate chacho sar mangel. Ando gova momento O Del akharda piro amal Brshind. Brshind astarda te perel pe Phuvjate. Gova locharda lache. O Thagar Kham na resla.

Sar o Thagar Kham, gadija o Thagar Chon astarda lesko plan e chehrajinenca. Numaj, ando momento kana o Chon akharda e chehrajine i Phuv bichalda sa Chirikle ando Del. O Del dija sama pala Chirikle thaj o Thagar Chon sasa bizo

7

reslipe.

Kana o Thagar Balval astarda te phurdel pe Phuvjate e
saste zuralesa, o Del ulada e Phuvjatar. Gova Balvalesko
phurdipe cherda buchi pala uladipe. Plano sasa cherdino.

Akana Deleske thaj Phuvjache pandz chavore astarile te
chingaren kon trubuj te achen e dejasa thaj kon trubuj te
dzal e dadesa. Chingaripe sasa dziko lenge dej Phuv na dĩja
vorba: "Tu, o Thagar Kham, tu o Thagar Chon, thaj tu o
Thagar Balval, tumen mudardile man. Nashen mandar! A tu,
e Thagarica Tunjariko Parnimata, thaj tu e Thagarica Jag, na
cherden man khanchi doshalo. Achen mansa!"

Kataro gova vakto o Del thaj e Phuv san ulade, thaj lenge
chavore dzuvden ando sajekhesko chingaripeste.

An Unusual Family

A long time ago, before there were people living on the earth, the Sky and the Earth were married very happily. They had five children. The first child was King Sun; the second King Moon; the third Queen Fire; the fourth King Wind; and the fifth Queen Fog.

These children quarreled constantly. Therefore, the Sky and the Earth decided to carve out a great, wide space and put their children in it. This angered their sons, who decided to take their revenge by creating problems between their parents.

The sons planned to separate their parents and cause them to divorce. Once separated, the children could each build separate castles for themselves.

King Sun said, "I am going to scorch Mother Earth with all my force. Mother cannot withstand my scorching power. If you, my brother Moon, do not take your turn in the sky, Mother Earth will burn away, separating from our Father Sky."

Then King Moon said, "While you scorch Mother Earth, I will turn to Father Sky and call out all the stars to surround him and take him away from our Mother Earth."

Finally, King Wind said, "I agree with both of you. I am going to blow with all my force and take our Father Sky away from her."

They were all in agreement, for once. First, the Sun King started his attack. He scorched Mother Earth exactly as he had planned. At that moment, however, Sky called his friend Rain, who helped soothe Mother Earth. Therefore, the Sun King did not succeed.

Like the Sun King, the Moon King tried his plan on Father Sky, surrounding Sky with all the stars. But at that moment, the Earth sent all the birds into the sky. Father Sky's attention was only upon the birds, not upon the stars, and so the Moon King did not succeed.

But when the Wind King used all his force on his mother, the Sky divided from the Earth.

Then, the children began to fight about who should stay with Mother Earth and who should stay with Father Sky. The fight lasted until Mother Earth declared, "You, King Sun, you King Moon, and you King Wind, you attacked me! Go away! But you, Queen Fog and Queen Fire, you did me no harm. You can stay with me!"

And ever since this time, sky and earth have been divided, and their children have squabbled constantly.

Sar o Devel Cherda e Rromen

Ando dumutnipeste e Devlese phanda pe godji te cheren o manush. Vov phenda korkoro peske: "Ako cherdam o Kham thaj o Chon, shaj te cherav o manush. Sose na?"

O Devel lelo o chik thaj astarda te cherel o kipo.

Kana gatisarda o kipo, vov thovda o kipo ando chiravdeste, thaj ande furnavate te peken les. Pala pekipe trubulo but sahati. O Devel djelo ande pashimata te phirel. Avri sasa but shukar, thaj o Devel bistarda o kipo. Kana avilo chere, o sasto kipo sasa kalo. O Devel na mangla te chuden les, thaj e Devlese phanda pe godji te dija e kipese o dzuvdipe. Vov phurda leske dzuvdipeske hava ando muj, thaj gova kipo astarda te phurdel. E kipestar iklada dzuvdo manush. Gova manush sasa majpurano kalo manush.

O Devel, pale, astarda te cherel nevo manush. Vov gatisarda e chikesko kipo, thaj thovda les ando chiravdeste, thaj ande furnavate te peken les. Numaj gova drom, o Devel sasa daravdo. Na djelo avri ando phiripeste. Vov na mangla te cherel pale sar cherda angluno drom. O Devel dija but sama pala gova kipo.

"Jekh sahato si dosta pala o kipo", gndisarda o Devel. So gndisarda, gadija cherda. O Devel lelo o kipo-manush andare furnavate. Gova kipo sasa sasto parno. Pale, pherde ilehko, o Devel na mangla te chudel o kipo-manush. Vov phurda e kipese lachi dzuvdipeski hava ando muj. Gova kipo astarda te phurdel. E kipestar iklada dzuvdo manush. Gova manush sasa majpurano parno manush.

"Trinto drom — trinto baxt, mora te avel but lacho, sumnakaj bojava manush", o Devel phenda korkoro peske. Vov

thovda nevo chikesko kipo-manush ando chiravdeste, thaj
ande furnavate te peken les. Vov dija bari sama. Na djelo ando
phiripeste. O Devel avel but azhucharno. Lesko azhucharipe
cherda lachi buchi. O Devel cherda but shukar, sumnakaj
bojava kipo thaj sasa but baxtalo pala gova. Vov phurda
leske e dzuvdipeski hava ando muj, phurda kamipe, phurda
hacharipe thaj sa Devlikano dzuvdipesko zumadipe. Thoska
o Devel phenda: "Tu trubuj te aves e Rromengo majpurano
manush!"

How God Made the Roma

A long time ago, God decided to create a man. He realized that, since He had made the sun and the moon, He would also be able to make a man. Therefore, God took some mud and started to make a clay statue of a man. When He was satisfied, He placed it in the oven to bake it. He figured the baking would take several hours, and when He became bored with waiting, He went for a walk to pass the time. Since the weather was beautiful, God forgot about the statue and, when He remembered it, He came back to find it had been in the oven for too long. The statue had baked for so long that it turned a black colour. Since God did not want to throw away this figure, He breathed life into it, and this first man became the ancestor of the Black People.

Then, God decided to create another man. He placed the clay statue into the oven for baking. This time, however, God stayed near the oven, because He did not want to bake the statue for too long. In His impatience, God removed the statue too soon, and it was a white colour. Because God did not want to throw away this figure, He breathed life into the statue and it became the ancestor of the White People.

God, then, tried a third time to form a man. When He finished kneading the clay figure and placed it in the oven, He had in mind a medium-brown man. God did not go for a walk this time, either, but stayed close to the oven. He was patient, too, this time, and His patience paid off. When God removed the clay figure from the oven, He saw a beautiful, brown-coloured man. He was proud of His work and he blew the breath of life, including life's experiences and emotions, into the new figure. God then decided that this man would become the ancestor of the Roma.

Rromano Princo Penga

Ando dumutnipeste dzivela zuralo Rromano Thagar Hrom. Rroma thaj lenge Rromano Thagar seha-len piri phuv, thaj von avile but baxtale. Sa e Rroma pari cherde pala lenge Thagar thaj savore seha-len barvalo dzuvdipe. Thagar Hrom seha-leh e chavoresko chavo, Rromano Princo Penga. Penga sasa doshalo, thaj sa so vov cherda, lesko garadino phral, pe akhardipe Bengo, xasajvilo lesa. Jekethane cherde but dilimata. Ando chachipeste Bengo sasa o beng. Von du-jende cherde o plano kana Thagar Hrom mulel, von ka dzan te bolden pe shoreha sa so sasa lache ande gova phuvjate. Von mangle te cheren sasto Rromano them but chororo thaj pocikno.

Thoska jekh brsh sa sasa sar duj dile seha-len ando plano. Rromano Thagar Hrom mula, thaj e phuvjako phiravipe lela Princo Penga. E Rroma na mangle les. Sa e Rroma dzanle kaj Penga thaj lesko dilo ratvalo- phral Bengo hi-len o plano te mudaren sa so si dzuvdo ande gova phuvjate. Sa e Rroma bandjavile e Devlese thaj e Lachache pala azhutipe. Von mora te dzuvden, pale, sar chache manusha.

Pengesko thaj Bengesko plan sasa: te cheren Rroma pocikne koring e Pengese, thaj te cheren len te pachaven e Penga sar von pachavile lesko phurodad. Numaj, gova plano sasa chachi, bari dilimata. Bengo avilo bilacho Pengesko mothodipesko manush. Sako chon Penga seha-leh nevi ideja te cherel neve doshalimata. Vov cherda but doshalipe: lelo Rromengo djiv, lelo lenge chavore thaj cherda lendar e mar-nala. Vov lelo sasto phuv. Bengo djelo ande familije bizo akharipe thaj phurda lendje nasvalipe, phurda mulo drab ande phuvjate, thaj lelo lendje dozacharipe.

Sa so cherda sasa pala Penga cira.

Vov seha-leh dujto plano. Vov mangla te cherel e Rromende but doshalipe. Akana, lesko plano sasa kaj, pala e Rromen musaj te avel nabistardesko, bendjalo vakto.

Penga dija buchi anglunese vojvodese, te cherel jekh Devleski cher kataro chiral thaj o goj, a naj sar aver Devleske chera kataro bar, cigla thaj malteri. Thaj, vojvoda cherda so Penga mangla.

Angluno, Rroma avile daravne te dzan kote, numaj bokhalipe thaj chororipe avile sajekh baredar. Von djele kote pala dozacharipe thaj pala hape.

Va, gova sasa Pengesko plan. Rroma avile kote sako djive, naj odolese kaj avile bare pachavne, numaj odolese kaj avile bokhale.

Penga dzangla kaj bokhale Rroma na shaj te azhucharen lungo. Lesko plano sasa: bokhale Rroma e bokhalipestar mora te astaren te han e Devlesko cher. Athoska, vov shaj te cherel so vov mangel thaj kamel.

Sako drom kana Rroma djele ando Devlesko cher, Penga dija e manushende vareso dipe. Vov dija sa so vov lendar lelo. Gova dipe sasa dziko khandjiri sasa pherdi. But Rroma avile kote thaj beshle avri opashin e Devlesko cher, odolese so ande khandjiri naj seha-leh o than.

Pindzardo si amaro pachape: ako vareko halo piro Devlesko cher, vov musaj te avel bibaxtalo, bokhalo thaj chororo pala sasto trajipe. Gova sasa Pengesko plan. Sako djive Rroma hale zala po zala chiral thaj goj, dziko xale sasto Devlesko cher.

Athoska Princo Penga mothoda e Rromendje kaj von mora te nashen andari phuvjate. Ako na, vov dzal te mudarel savore. But milionura Rroma nashadile.

Numaj, Lachi thaj Devel dikhle so sasa pe phuvjate. Von na kamle so Princo Penga cherda e Rromende. Lachi thaj Devel cherde o kris te azhutinen lendje, Rromendje.

Devel cherda o baro bar e Pengestar.

Ande gova situacija naj avilo vareko shajipe te akharen nashavde Rroma te dzan chere, te irisaren ando them.

Lachi djeli pe dromeste te avel sajekh e Rromenca. Voj si e Rromenca kana von trubuj arakhipe. Kaj Rroma, kate Lachi.

Devel dikhla kaj Lachake odji thaj lako pherdo ilo achile e Rromenca, thaj vov cherda o kris te avel lenca, Rromenca, e chache thaj lache manushenca.

Kataro gova vakto Rroma sajekh e darasa phenden kataro Penga. Pengeske odji si sajekh pe phuvjate dujto Augusto kana Rroma baxtaren o Aldjun.

Penga izdrarel Rroma. Penga izdrarel sako cher. Dziko opashodjive Penga thaj Ilija (Bengo) san jekhethane. Dziko opashodjive Rroma bakre chinen. E Rromnja cheren pogacha ande jagesko praxo. Sako Rrom mora te cherel o hape dziko Alija na astarel te cherel bashalipe. Athoska, pala sastipe von tataren prna pe jagate.

Pala dopashodjive, kana Pengeske thaj Ilijeske odja nashaven, Rroma chelen thaj djilaben e Alijasa.

Romani Prince Penga

A long time ago, there lived a powerful Romani king called Hrom. He ruled over a Romani country where all the Roma lived contentedly in their own state. All the Roma respected King Hrom. They had plenty of food to eat, and they were at peace.

King Hrom had a grandson called Prince Penga. Penga had an adopted brother named Beng. Beng was a devil whose influence over Penga was very powerful. Penga and Beng made a secret plan: as soon as King Hrom died, they would destroy all the good things he had accomplished in the country during his reign, and they would make all the Roma poor and humble.

After a year had passed, King Hrom died, and Prince Penga became the ruler of the land. The Roma did not love Penga as they had loved Hrom: they prayed to Devel, the Romani God, and to Lachi, the Goddess of Good, that they might help the Roma survive Penga's tyranny. They prayed to the gods because they believed that Penga and his adopted brother Beng would exterminate everybody in the land.

Prince Penga and Beng wanted to make everybody in the country completely dependent upon them, to force the people to admire and love them as much as they had loved King Hrom. But this plan did not work. Beng was a bad advisor, and he told Penga to introduce more and more laws that would anger the Roma and make their lives more difficult. He told Penga to take away the corn grown by the people; to take away their sons to become soldiers; to confiscate their houses and property. Moreover, Penga also visited their homes without being invited, and he spread sickness among them. He poisoned the earth itself, and he took away all the people's hope. Realizing that Beng's plans were failing, Penga then resolved himself to a new plan against the Roma people.

Penga called up his first voivode, a wealthy boss, and told him to build a church made of cheese and sausages instead of brick and stone. The voivode did so. This was Penga's plan: to force the Roma to attend church regularly, not just because they worshipped God but because they were starving. He knew that their hunger would soon drive them to eat their own church. This would, Penga knew, force the people into even greater hardship than before.

At first, the Roma were afraid to attend this church, but because they were poor and hungry, they did attend. Their hope was soon rewarded: every time they attended this church, Penga gave them back something he had stolen from them. This continued until Penga was sure that everybody was attending regularly. Then, one day, when the church and surrounding land were crowded with worshippers, Penga took away everything he had given back to them. The Roma were, once again, starving and attended the church only to eat the cheese and sausage.

There is a belief that people who eat their churches will become cursed by God and will become miserable, hungry, and poor. This was Penga's vision for Roma. Every day, the people ate more cheese and sausage and, in a matter of time, they ate the entire church.

Now Prince Penga told the Roma that they had become cursed for eating their church and that, if they did not leave the country, he would kill all of them. Millions of Roma left the lands. But Devel, the Romani God, and the Goddess Lachi watched over them. They did not approve of Penga's evil ways and what he had done to his people, so they decided to help the Roma. God cursed Penga and turned him into a stone. But it was impossible to gather all the Roma back to their homeland where they had suffered so much because of Penga. So, the Goddess Lachi decided to stay with the Roma and protect them wherever they happened to be in the world. When Devel saw that Lachi loved the Roma and had decided to stay with them and help them, He decided to stay with Her to help them too.

Ever since then, the Roma have been afraid to talk about Prince Penga. Many Roma believe that every second of August, when they celebrate Aldjun Day, Penga's spirit walks over the earth with his evil companion, Ilija. He shakes houses and terrifies the Roma inside. Penga and Ilija force the host to prepare food until, at noon, Alija, a good spirit, begins to play music, driving Penga and Ilija from the earth.

On the day of Aldjun, the Roma families sacrifice a sheep to Penga and divide the meat among everybody for the feast. Then, the hostess of each house prepares "pogacha", un-leavened bread, and bakes it in the ashes of a communal fire. Afterwards, the Roma warm their feet around this fire, believing it will bring them health.

At noon, when Alija is playing music, Penga and Ilija must leave the earth, and the Roma dance and celebrate to honour Alija.

Karankochi-Kochi

Athoska e Rromenge tradimatako, o Rromano Princo Penga sasa cherdino ando baro bar, thaj amare Rroma dzivina opashin saste lumijate. Von dzivina sar njama, saranda dziko shovvardesh familijengo jekhethane. Gova sasa jekhoro drom pala Rromengoro dzuvdipe. Lachi thaj Devel avile e Rromenca pe lenge dromeste te azhutinen lendje ando nasvalipeste thaj bokhalipeste. Numaj, kote avile thaj varese bahvaljake save tradile len. Varese bahvaljake avile lache, varese dzungale.

Me dzav te phendav tumenge jekh paramichi kataro dzungalo bahvalj pe akhardipe Karankochi-Kochi.

Karankochi-Kochi sajekh rodel o dzeno savo si but godjaverno, savo si bizhavno, te cherel lestar o baro dilo. Ako Karankochi-Kochi cherel jekh dzeno ando vareko njamo sar o baro dilo, vov sajekh avel kote ando njamo dziko na xal sa so si but barikano pala Rromen thaj lendje dzuvdipe.

Bahvalj Karankochi-Kochi cherdel pes ando chaglo manush – mindilici, balalo pe sasto mujeste thaj trupeste. Vov si but zuralo, pinda centimeturja vucho, thaj hi-leh loli stadji pe shoreste.

Majpalo drom Karankochi-Kochi avilo ando vakto kana dzivela mardo Alija. Alija sasa but bizhavno manush. Karankochi-Kochi cherda lestar o dilo, thaj lela lesko Hopo thaj Dopo. Ando gova vakto Alija achilo bizo sumnakaj thaj bizo bendjali stadji.

Gova drom Karankochi-Kochi mangla te avel ande Mejrako cher. Mejra sasa e Alijeski chej. Thoska e babosko meripe Lachi dija e Mejrache bendjali Trasta te azhutinen e njamese ande chororipeste. Thaj Karankochi-Kochi mangla gova Mejraki bendjali Trasta.

Mejra sasa zurali, bidaraki, vuchi thaj chishli, e lunge

parne bala thaj kale jakha, phuri Rromni. Voj sasa but bizhavni Rromni. Ande chachipe, Mejra sasa lachi, bidaraki "Phuri dej". Trasta thaj Mejra avile majlache amalina. Trasta vacharda lasa thaj dija lache mishte turvinjipa. Trasta thaj Mejra avile sajekh perde: but hape, pipe, sheja... Sa familija dzivela e Mejratar thaj e Trastatar.

Mejraki mahala achili chorori ando vakto kana Karankochi-Kochi cherda o dilo e Alijastar. Ando gova vakto Karankochi-Kochi andothan sumnakaj opashin Rromani mahala cherda thaj mukla grastengo khul thaj chororipe. Sasto njamo dzangla so sasa.

Rroma ande mahala dzangle kaj Karankochi-Kochi trubul te avel pale te dikhel Mejra thaj te lel laki bendjali Trasta. Ali von na dzangle kana. Phuri dej Mejra azhucharda gova maladipe. Voj dzangla so shaj thaj trubuj te cherel.

Jekh rach kana chehrajina dije strafin pe Mejraki mahala, Karankochi-Kochi cherda o kris te dzal pe phuvjate. Vov avilo ande Mejrako cher. Karankochi-Kochi dija andre krzo thuvalo. Mejra vazdindja. Voj ashunisarda vareko chingaripe ando sulundaro.

Tra-ta-ta- thaj hooopa- andothan kate avilo Karankochi-Kochi. Mejra dzangla so trubuj te cherel e ciknese, dzungalese manushese. Voj dzangla sar te marel les, e odjesa thaj e zuralesa.

Karankochi-Kochi bandjisarda e Mejrache sar koring e thagaricache thaj phenda:

"O tu, Mejra, me pachav tut. Tu san bidaravni, bizhavni Rromni. Me dzanav kaj sa e Rroma pachaven tut. Me dzanav gachi kames tuche Trasta, thaj so tu e Trastenca cheres pala chiro njamo. Ashun, hi-man jekh rudjipe. Me ka dav tut miri loli stadji. Bendjali, loli stadji shaj te cherel sa so tu manges, thaj tu thaj chiri familija shaj te dzuvden ando barvalipeste. Trin dromengo mora te mudares e stadjesa pe podo, thaj trin dromengo musaj te phendes: 'Karankochi-Kochi, de ma but sumnakaj,' thaj bendjali, loli stadji ka cherel so tu manges. Pala gova me mangav chiri Trasta. Le! Le stadji!"

Sigo, vov dija e Mejrache piri stadji. Thaj, ando momento

kote sasa bari, balali Karankochi-Kochesko shoro. Vov gndisarda: "Mejra dzal te avel daravni kana dikhel mrno shoro."

Numaj vov sasa cira daravno thaj sar cherdino ando bar
kana dikhel Mejrako lacho, bidaravno muj. Mejra lija i stadji
thaj cherda so Karankochi-Kochi vacharda. Sasa lacho. Kote
sasa but sumnakaj, sar piramida but sumnakaj. Voj cherda
efta piramida. Sar vachardo, gadija cherdino. Mejra dija
Trasta e Karankochi- Kochese, numaj voj seha-la jekh plano.
Voj dzangla kaj Karankochi-Kochi musaj te dzal pe deleste
dziko teharin, angla o kham ikljovel. Mejra dzangla kaj vov
dzal te cherel latar o dilo pala leski stadji. Loli stadji cherda
pala Mejra but sumnakaj, thaj Mejrache mangipen cherde pe
ando chachipe. Ande Mejrate chereste sa sasa e sumnakajestar. Sasto cher strafindja e sumnakajestar. Zidurja avile
sumnale, thuvalo thaj sulundaro sumnalo. Mejrache coha,
gad, parno bal, danda thaj vundje avile e sumnakajestar.

Mejra, lachi, bizhavni Rromni, dzangla sar te lundjarel o
Devlesko vakto dziko o kham ikljovel.

Kana o kham iklovel Karankochi-Kochi musaj te nashavel.
Mejra djeli sigo dziko udareste, mangla te nashaven e stadjesa,
numaj ando momento Karankochi-Kochi sasa kote. Vov lelo
jekh stadjako kotor, dziko aver kotor icharda Mejra. Liduj
mudarde thaj cherde chingaripe sar pala o dzuvdipe.

Pe stinge rigate – pe chache rigate, pe chache rigate – pe
stinge rigate, von crde jekh aver. Blamp- von pherde talo pe
podo thaj cherde but chingara kaj tumen nashti te pachaven.

Hoopaa- chingaripe sasa zuralo pala liduj, thaj stadji
pharada. Mejra thaj Karankochi-Kochi pherde tele pe duj
rigate.

Karankochi-Kochi seha-leh stadji ande leske va.

Vov mangla sigo te nashen odolese so kham astarda te
ikljovel. Vov na dikhla kaj jekh stadjaki kotor achili e Mejrasa.
Karankochi-Kochi bistarda Trasta. Vov mudarda e stadjesa
trin dromengo pe podo thaj vacharda:" Neka gova sumnakaj
avel grastengo khul", thaj nashada krzo sulundari, krzo thuv-
jalo, dziko thaneste katar vov avilo.

Mejra achili jakhali kana dikhla sar sumnakaj bandjavda

ando grastengo khul. Ando momento voj dikhla lachi Trasta. E jasvenca thaj e kamipesa dija angali e Trastache. Mejra thovda e stadjache kotor ande Trasta, thaj chindili beshlja pe cheresko hudumich – prago. Voj azhutisarda aver Rroma te vazden. E godjasa sar phandi voj djeli andre ande chereste. Mangla kafava te pijel, thaj chiravda kafava. Uzo furnava pe zido sasa dikhlo. Mejra dikhla ando dikhlo thaj, so. . .

Mejrake danda achile e sumnakajestar. Laki coha, gad, angrustika, cheja, lancurja, merikle achile e sumnakajestar. Ando momento, voj dikhla sar vareso strafinel ande soba. Talo grastengo khul sasa sumnakaj. Sumnakaj strafindja. Voj chuda e grastengo khul thaj talo saki piramida dikhla efta dukatengo. E Mejrache pherda pe godji kaj shaj te avel, te loli, bendjali pharadi stadji shaj te cherel pale sumnakaj. Karankochi-Kochi na cherda lachi buchi thaj na cherda e Mejrache phuri dili. Na sasto. Voj lela stadjache kotor andare Trasta thaj astarda te mudarel pe podo: "Karankochi-Kochi, dema but sumnakaj." Bloompaaaaaaaa — gova cherda buchi.

Kote na sasa bari sumnakuni piramida, ali sako drom kana Mejra phuchla e stadjache kotor pala o sumnakaj, kote avile efta dukati. Voj phuchla saranda thaj shtar dromengo. Ande mahala san saranda thaj shtar familije. Saki familija trubuj pale gasavo, pala saki familija efta dukatengo. Kataro gova vakto Mejra cherel sumnakaj numaj kana si ande mahala bari kriza.

Lachi Trasta thaj e stadjake kotor idjarda Mejraki chavoreski chej, Mejra.

Amen dozacharen kaj terni Mejra dzanel so trubul te cherel kana Karankochi-Kochi pale avel te lel Trasta thaj bendjalo stadjako kotor ando gova mardesko njamo.

Achen Devleha mrne Rromalen!

Karankochi-Kochi

When God turned evil Prince Penga to stone after the Roma were forced to flee their own country, the Roma were dispersed throughout several countries all over the world. They lived in groups of forty to sixty families, for this was the only way to survive the poverty they were forced to endure. Since the exile of the Roma, Lachi, the Goddess of Good, and Devel, the Romani God, had followed them and protected them from illness and starvation. Some spirits followed the Roma, too. Some of these spirits were good and some were evil. I will now relate the legend of a spirit called Karankochi-Kochi.

Karankochi-Kochi always seeks the wisest and most intelligent of the Romani community so that he can make a fool of this person. When he has fooled someone in a group, he continues to play his tricks until he has stolen everything of value to the group's survival.

Karankochi-Kochi is an ugly man covered with long hair all over his body. He is fifty centimeters tall, very strong, and always wears a red cap.

On one of his previous visits to Earth, Karankochi-Kochi appeared during the lifetime of the very good and wise blacksmith, Alija. Karankochi-Kochi had promised Alija vast sums of gold by the magic of his red cap. Instead, he tricked Alija and stole his hammer and anvil, and he also stole all the gold from the community. After that, the community was destitute, for all of their gold was turned to manure by Karankochi-Kochi.

On his next visit, Karankochi-Kochi appeared in the house of Mejra. She was the daughter of Alija, and she had a large magic bag (her Trasta) given to her by the Goddess Lachi to protect the Romani ghetto after Alija's death. Mejra was considered "Phuri Dej", an old wise woman among the Roma. She was very brave, tall and slim with long grey hair and dark eyes. She had inherited her right to lead the community from her father. The Trasta was her friend, and she could talk to this bag. It always gave her good advice. Whenever Mejra went out with her Trasta, she never returned empty-handed. Her whole family depended on her work, since the ghetto suffered great poverty from the time Karankochi-Kochi fooled Alija. Everybody knew how the spirit had tricked the blacksmith and had stolen from the community. The people also knew that, one day, Karankochi-Kochi would return to visit Mejra and try to trick her, too, and steal her Trasta. But Mejra was prepared for the evil spirit.

One night, when all the stars were bright, Karankochi-Kochi decided to visit Mejra's home. He entered through the chimney. The noise woke Mejra, and she saw Karankochi-Kochi standing inside her house. She was not surprised, and she was ready to get the better of this ugly spirit. She decided to show him that she was smarter than he, and that she was ready to fight him using her considerable physical and intellectual strength. The spirit approached Mejra and took a deep bow. He said to her, "Mejra, I honour you as a brave and wise woman. I know how much everyone respects you. I also know how much your Trasta means to you and to your family. Let us, then, make an agreement. I am going to give you my magic cap. This cap will do anything that you ask of it. You and your family can live abundantly. All you have to do is to strike the floor three times with this magic cap and say, 'Karankochi-Kochi, give me a lot of gold!' Then, the cap will give you the gold. In exchange, you must give me your Trasta. Let us try it. Here, take my cap!"

In a flash, Karankochi-Kochi removed his red cap and appeared before her quite large, hairy and terrifying. He thought that his change of appearance would frighten Mejra. But she simply stood there, relaxed and unaffected, and it was Karankochi-Kochi who was instead surprised. Mejra took the cap and did as the ugly spirit had instructed: she struck the cap on the floor three times and asked for gold, and suddenly there appeared seven piles of gold on the floor.

After that, Karankochi-Kochi asked Mejra to give him her Trasta. She surrendered her magic bag because she had crafted a cunning plan. She knew that Karankochi-Kochi would leave the Earth before sunrise and that he would do everything in his power to make a fool of her by reclaiming his red cap. Mejra continued asking the cap for things, and everything she asked for appeared before her. Everything in her home glittered because it had all turned to gold. The walls were golden; the chimney and coal scuttle, too. Even Mejra's blouse, skirt, and grey hair turned golden, and her teeth and nails too! But she knew this was not the end of the story. Soon it would be sunrise and time for Karankochi-Kochi to leave. So, Mejra ran out of the house with the red cap in her hands. Karankochi-Kochi gave chase, trying to steal the cap away from her. He grabbed a corner of it, and they both pulled and tugged. They were both strong and as they fought over the cap, they fell onto the ground with a loud crash. During their struggle, the cap tore in half: Karankochi-Kochi was in such a hurry to leave that he did not realize he held only one half of the red cap in his hands. Furthermore, the struggle caused him to be very late, and in his hurry he forgot all about the Trasta. As Karankochi-Kochi climbed to the top of the chimney, he hit the floor three times with his half of the magic cap and said, "Change this gold into manure!"

When Karankochi-Kochi had vanished up the chimney, Mejra was astonished to see that all her gold turned to manure. Then she saw her Trasta that Karankochi-Kochi had forgotten. She picked it up and held it as if it were a baby. She put her half of the magic cap into the Trasta and went to sit just outside her door, waiting for the rest of the community to awaken.

After waiting, she grew thirsty, so she went back inside to prepare her morning coffee. On her way to the stove, she glanced at her reflection in the mirror and saw that she had golden teeth. Her skirt and blouse were also golden, and she still had all the gold jewelry she had asked for. Then she saw something else: there was gold shining from under the manure in the seven piles upon the floor. She brushed away the manure and she found seven gold ducats in each stack. She now realized that Karankochi-Kochi's magic was only half as powerful as he thought it was, since he possessed only half of his magic cap. Mejra retrieved her half of the cap from her Trasta and tried to make more gold. She discovered that the half-cap was still powerful! The cap did not give her pyramids of gold like before, but it did give her seven gold ducats every time she asked. She asked the cap, therefore, to give her seven gold ducats for each of the forty-four families living in her ghetto. Since this time, Mejra has used her half of the magic cap to ask for seven gold ducats whenever her family needed money. Her granddaughter, also called Mejra, inherited the torn half of the magic cap as well as the Trasta, and everybody hopes that young Mejra will be well-prepared when Karankochi-Kochi decides to return.

Shtarto Kafrin

Kana Isus sasa dino e Rimskake karnalende te inzaren les pe trushuleste, duj karnalengo rode shtar kafrinengo, thaj djele ko angluno mardo te cheren len. Mardo sasa phuro Dzungo. Kana vov ashundja sose von trubuj e kafrina, vov na mangla te cherel len. Odolese, e karnala thovde lesko cher ando jag thaj mudardile les.

Karnale djele te phuchen dujto mardo. Mardo astarda te marel sastri, numaj kana ashundilo sose von trubuj e kafrina, na mangla te cheren len. Andothan, o mardo thaj karnale ashundile o krlo e mudardese mardese: "Arija-amal, na cher e kafrina, von mangen te inzaren o manush savo si amaro phral."

Kana karnale ashundile gova krlo von daravde nashadile.

Karnale djele dur te roden o mardo savo trubul te cheren e kafrina. Ande Jerusalemeske opashinate von maladile jekh Rrom pe anav Redzo. Redzo cherda peske cahra thaj opash cahra thovda hopo, dopo thaj aver alat. Vov astarda te cherel e kafrina.

Kana gatisarda trin kafrina, karnale mothodile sose trubuj len. Ando palo momento von ashundile o krlo e mudardese mardese: "Arija- amal, na cher e kafrina, von mangen te inzaren o manush savo si amaro phral."

Kana karnale ashundile gova krlo von daravde nashadile.

Daravno Redzo astarda te cherel shtarto kafrin te gatisarel gova buchi. Kana thovda o paj prdal pe kafrinesko, kafrin achilo phabardo. Vov pale thovda but paj, kafrin achilo pale phabardo. Akana thovda but paj, andothan o shtarto kafrin astarda te phabarel sa xalo than. Vov na gatisarda buchi. Vov na gatisarda shtarto kafrin.

Redzo daravdo nashada e cahrasa. Vov nashada krzo

but thana dziko chindilo thaj sovljardo perda tele thaj sutla. Ando suno Redzo xacharda vareso tato talo prnalende, thaj andothan avilo dzungado.

Kate sasa tato, jagalo kafrin. Vov zumavda te achavel o kafrin numaj sasa bizo reslipe.

Paramichi vacharel kaj si o kafrin sajekh mashkaro e Rromende ande mardeske familijate. Odolese mardeske familije sajekh phiraven kataro jekh than dziko aver than. Godova shtarto kafrin savo trubul te avel pala e Isusesko inzaripe phiravel e Rromenca pe themeste.

The Fourth Nail

When Jesus was condemned to be crucified by the Romans, two Roman soldiers were detailed to bring four nails for this crucifixion. They went to the first blacksmith nearby and ordered him to make four nails. When the blacksmith, who was an old Jew, found out what the nails were for, he refused to forge them.

The two soldiers burned the blacksmith's beard, and then they stabbed him to death with a spear. They soon found another blacksmith and they asked him to forge the four nails. When the blacksmith heard what the nails were for, he stopped working. At that moment, he heard the voice of the murdered blacksmith telling him, "Aria, do not forge the nails. Those nails are going to be used to crucify an innocent Jew."

The soldiers were frightened by the voice, and they ran away. Outside of Jerusalem, the soldiers found Alija, a Romani blacksmith, who was putting up his tent and setting up his anvil. Following the soldiers' orders, Alija started to forge the nails. He finished three before the soldiers told him what the nails were for. At that moment, they all heard the voice of the murdered blacksmith once again, and this frightened the soldiers so that they ran away.

Alija decided to finish his job anyway, and he started to forge the fourth nail. When he poured water over the nail to temper and cool it, the water vanished and the nail glowed red hot. Alija poured more water on it, but the nail became brighter and hotter, illuminating the entire desert.

Alija was terrified. He packed his tent, took his belongings, and he travelled far away until his exhaustion forced him to sleep. The glowing nail appeared beside his leg and it burned him while he slept. Alija woke and poured water on the wound to cool it, but nothing would soothe the mark.

According to legend, the nail still appears to the black-smith's descendants. This is why they move from one place to another. The fourth nail, intended for Christ's crucifixion, follows the Roma wherever they travel.

Sumnalo Vasil

Kana o Devel cherda nevo them, vov dija o kriso te thovel duj thema ando tangipeste, pharipeste thaj mangla te dikhel lenge vodja. Gova avile Rroma thaj Dzuge.

Angluno, o Devel phuchla e Dzuge te dzan pe jekh baro drom. Von trubul te dzan krzo lungo drom kaj avilo baro paj. Ando chachipe gova sasa baro dorjav. Pe gova dromeste e Dzuge trubul te cheren bari lachimata pala o Devel. Von na daradile e pajestar. E Dzuge avile lache jekh e averenca, thaj e reslipensa djele krzo drom thaj nakhadile. Von achile dzuvde.

Thoska, pale gasavo trubul te cheren e Rroma. Rroma avile daravde e pajestar. Sar sajekh, i gova drom Rroma avile bisigarne thaj Devel cherda o chelipe lenca. Vov thovda baro paj opral len te tasajven len. Numaj, jekh Sumnalo pe anav Vasil dikhla gova, thaj kovljardilo pala e Rromen. Vov djelo te dikhel thaj phendel e Devlesa pala azhutipe thaj cira dozacharipe pala e Rromen. Numaj, o Devel na ashundilo so phenda Sumnalo Vasil. Devel na kamlja leske.

Sumnalo Vasil gndisarda kaj mora te rodel aver drom te azhutinel e Rromendje. Vasil akharda e Devleske papine te urjaven opral o baro paj thaj inklaven e Rromen andaro daravno pajestar. Thaj, papine inklavile len.

Rroma nakhadile. Rroma achile dzuvde.

Kataro gova vakto, kana o Sumnalo Vasil thaj e papine inkladisarde amare Rroma andaro pajestar, astardilo nevo dzuvdipe pala sa Rroma ando gova them. Gova djive si ando deshoshtarto Januaro.

Gova paramichi dzuvdel dziko adjive mashkaro e Rromen ando sasto them. Rachako angla deshoshtarto Januaro Rroma xan e papina, thaj cheren najisipe e Sumnalese Vasilese pala leske shukareske vodji. Sa e Rroma baxtaren e alavenca: "Baxtali Vasilica."

Saint Basil

When God created the world, He decided to sew strife between two nations, to test their mettle. Those two nations were the Roma and the Jews.

First, God asked the Jews to walk through a path He had created in the sea. They must go from one side of the sea to the other, along this path. The Jews were very well-organized and they quickly succeeded in traversing the sea. They survived.

Then, God gave the same task to the Roma. The Roma, however, were a little slower, and so God decided to play a trick on them: He closed the sea over the Roma.

Only one saint in Heaven witnessed this event, and this saint took pity on the Roma. This was Saint Basil. Saint Basil approached and spoke with God, asking God to take pity on the Roma and not to drown them. But God did not heed the saint, for He did not like Saint Basil. Therefore, Basil decided to save the Roma, himself. He asked all the geese in Heaven to fly over the sea and collect the Roma from the dangerous waters. The geese granted this request, and the Roma survived.

Since then, new life begins for the Roma every January 14th, the day they were saved by the geese of Saint Basil.

This legend survives to this day in Romani communities all over the world. On the eve of January 13th, the people sacrifice geese to Saint Basil for his kindness and goodwill. All Roma congratulate each other with the words, "Baxtalo bango Vasili" and "Baxtali Vasilica" which means "May Saint Basil bring you luck."

Shtar Phrala

Jekhvaratar avile shtar chorore phrala: Ramo, Yanko, Redzo thaj Lolo. Ramo sasa majphuro thaj dija vorba kaj trubul te dzal te rodel buchi. Vov phendja kana cherel but love thaj barvalipe vov mangel te akharel aver phrala te trajen jekhethane.

Sar angluno djelo Ramo. Vov djelo, djelo, thaj kana perda chindilo, beshlo uzo jekh vosheste thaj sutla.

Andothan, avilo cikno, dilo thaj zuralo manush, e parnesa shoresa, thaj phenda:

"Ushti, ushti, naj si lacho te soves kana si o parno djive. Ushti, tu bibucharno! Ushti!" Ramo dikhla gova dilo thaj phenda: "Me phiravav pe themeste te rodav buchi. Amen shtar phrala san but chorore."

Parno chor manush phenda:

"Shaj te azhutinav tut. Ako irisares jekh garadini godji, me ka dav tut but sumnakaj thaj love. Ashun gova garadini godji:

> Jekh kash, shtar zhicurja, jekh rovli,
> But djivengo,
> Naj si dzuvdo, bashalel thaj djilabel.
> So si gova?"

Ramo gndisarda, gndisarda, numaj na dzangla irisaripe.

Parno chor manush sasa cikno, ali but zuralo. But zuralo kaj khonik nashti te hacharel gova zuralipe. Parno chor mothoda leske irisaripe.

Irisaripe pe garadine vodji sasa "e chemane". Cikno manush mudarda les thaj cherda lestar lesko sluga - pocikno.

Athoska vareko vrjamo trin phrala na dzangle so desisajlo e Ramese. Yanko dija vorba kaj vov mangel te dzal te rodel o Ramo. Yanko djelo thaj phirdja pe palo drom savo phirdja o phral Ramo. Kana avilo dziko palo gasavo vosheste, vov pherda chindilo thaj sutla.

Andothan, avilo cikno, dilo thaj zuralo manush, e parnensa shorensa, thaj phenda:

"Ushti, ushti, naj si lacho te soves kana si o parno djive. Ushti, tu bibucharno! Ushti!"

Yanko dikhla gova dilo thaj phenda:

"Me phiravav pe themeste te rodav buchi. Amen phrala san but chorore."

Parno chor manush phendel: "Me shaj te azhutinav tut. Ako irisares jekh garadini godji, me ka dav tut but sumnakaj thaj love. Ashun gova garadini godji:

Kate si dzukel, bizo prnengo jal bizo chibesko
Ako si tut dzukela ande va
o dzukel chingarel,
ako thoves o dzukel pe phuvjate,
o dzukel si muto.
So si gova?"

Yanko godjaverel, godjaverel numaj na dzanol irisaripe.

Irisaripe sasa "o lanco". Cikno, zuralo manush cherda lestar lesko sluga.

Athoska varegachi chonengo o Redzo dija vorba e Lolesa kaj musaj te dzal te rodel Ramo thaj Yanko. Vov djelo pe palo gasavo drom sar duj phrala, thaj kana avilo dziko palo gasavo vosheste, pherda chindilo thaj sutla. Thaj, sar desisajlo e duj phralenca, desisajlo leske.

Andothan, avilo cikno, dilo thaj zuralo manush, e parnensa shorensa, thaj phenda:

"Ushti, ushti, naj si lacho te soves kana si o parno djive. Ushti, tu bibucharno! Ushti!"

Redzo dikhla gova dilo thaj phenda:

"Me phiravav pe themeste te rodav buchi. Amen phrala san but chorore."

Parno chor manush phenda: "Me shaj te azhutinav tut. Ako irisares jekh garadini godji, me ka dav tut but sumnakaj thaj love. Ashun gova garadini godji:

> Duj phrala dzan pasha o them.
> Sa manusha dikhen len.
> Numaj, phrala na dikhen jekh aver.
> So si gova?"

Redzo na dzangla irisaripe thaj pale gasavo desisajlo lasa sar e leske phralenca. Vov na dzangla irisaripe pe garadini godji savo sasa "o chon thaj o kham". Cikno, dilo thaj zuralo manush cherda lestar lesko sluga.

Akana majterno phral Lolo avilo pherdoilesko. Lolo na dzangla so sasa e phralenca. Ando vakto kana o trin phrala djele pe dromeste, vov seha-leh neve amala: o richi, o ruv thaj e barepojrachi. Lolo djelo e amalenca te rodel Ramo, Yanko thaj Redzo. Kana avilo dziko pala gasavo vosheste, vov pherda chindilo thaj sutla.

Leske amala, o richi, o ruv thaj e barepojrachi, djele ando vosheste te roden hape.

Andothan, avilo cikno, dilo thaj zuralo manush, e parnensa shorensa, thaj phenda:

"Ushti, ushti, naj si lacho te soves kana si o parno djive. Ushti, tu bibucharno! Ushti!"

Lolo dikhla gova dilo thaj dija vorba:

"Me phiravav pe themeste te rodav buchi. Amen phrala san but chorore."

Parno chor manush phenda: "Me shaj te azhutinav tut. Ako irisares jekh garadini godji, me ka dav tut but sumnakaj thaj love. Ashun gova garadini godji:

> Bojava sar o praxo, bizo agor, lungi linija,
> dzal krzo sa lumija.
> So si gova?"

Lolo irisarda "E droma". Gova sasa chacho irisaripe. Numaj, cikno manush astarda te mudarel o Lolo.

Lolo akharda pire amala thaj von mudardile o dilo, zuralo manush.

Terno Lolo djelo ando vosheste thaj roda leske phrala. Vov chinda e phralenge lancurja, thaj jekhethane rode but love, sumnakaj thaj barvalipe. Shtar phrala: Ramo, Yanko, Redzo thaj Lolo avile but barvale manusha.

Four Brothers

Once upon a time there lived four very poor brothers: Ramo, Yanko, Redzo and Lolo.

One day, Ramo told his brothers he would do something about their poverty: he would travel around the world to look for a job. He promised that, if he became rich, he would come back for them and share his wealth.

Ramo travelled almost halfway around the world. When he came to a forest, he felt tired and decided to take a rest. Then, from the forest came a small magician sporting a long white beard. He told Ramo, "Wake up! It isn't good to sleep during the day! You are lazy man. Wake up!"

Ramo got up and answered, "I have been travelling around the world to find a job to end my family's poverty."

The white-bearded man promised to help him. He promised Ramo a heap of gold and silver if he could answer the following riddle:

"One wood, four bows,
One stick, a lot of grains,
It isn't alive, it plays and it sings.
What is it?"

Ramo didn't know the answer to this riddle, so the magician revealed the answer: the violin.

Now, the white-bearded magician was a small man, but he was so powerful that he astonished Ramo beyond belief. Because of his ignorance, Ramo was beaten every day, and he became the magician's slave.

Back at home, the other brothers were worried about Ramo. Therefore, Yanko next made the decision to go around the world to look for a job. When he came to the same forest where the magician had found Ramo, Yanko fell into a deep sleep. Then the white-bearded man appeared and promised Yanko the same gold and silver if only Yanko could answer the following riddle:

> "There is a dog without legs or a tongue.
> If you take him into your hands,
> The dog rattles; if you put him on the earth,
> The dog is silent.
> What is it?"

Yanko could not give an answer, and so the white-bearded man revealed it: a chain. The magician then made Yanko, too, his slave.

Back at home, a few months had passed and Redzo told Lolo of his fear that something was wrong. Either the missing brothers had become rich and forgotten their family, or something terrible had happened to them while they travelled around the world.

Therefore, Redzo set out along the same path as his brothers, hoping to find them. When he came to the same forest, he fell asleep and the same white-bearded man woke him up and promised him the same gold and silver if he could answer the following riddle:

> "Two brothers are going around the world,
> All people see them,
> But the brothers can't see each other.
> Who are they?"

Because Redzo couldn't answer the riddle, the white-bearded man revealed the answer: the moon and the sun. Then he made Redzo his slave, too.

After some time, the fourth brother, Lolo, decided to go searching for his brothers. While he had been waiting for them, he became good friends with a bear, a wolf and a fox. Lolo's animal friends travelled along with him, and when Lolo became tired and had to take a rest, his friends went into the forest to find food. Then the white-bearded magician appeared and promised him gold and silver if he could answer the following riddle:

"Grey, endless, long lines,
are spread around the earth,
What is it?"

Lolo answered: The Roads. This was, indeed, the correct answer. He asked the magician for the promised gold and silver, but the white-bearded man started to beat Lolo instead. Lolo whistled, and his friends the bear, the wolf and the fox came to rescue him. They tore the white-bearded man to pieces and then released the other three brothers. The four brothers, Ramo, Yanko, Redzo and Lolo, then became very rich men.

Romana Bijandili Richini

Angla dur vakto dzivela terni Rromani chej pe akhardipe Romana. Romana sasa but shukar thaj knonik na pachavda kaj si govathemeski chej. Sa manushen gndisarde kaj Romana sasa e Devleski sumnali chej. Romana sasa but lachi thaj bipharadi.

Voj sasa lachi koring e manushende, koring e dzuvljendje, koring e chavorende, koring e voshtake shingalende, thaj koring e chiriklendje.

Numaj, lache desisajlo vareso so khonik nashti te hacharel thaj pachavel. Voj khamnisarda, ali na sutla e Rromesa. Gova sasa baro ladzavipe pala las thaj pala laki familija. Ichardegodjaki Romana phirda pe dorjaveste te tasajvel pes.

Kana avili dziko dorjaveste, o paj achilo te nashel lendar. Romana sasa biazhuchardi thaj daradi. Voj zumada te tasavel pes pale thaj pale. Kana voj djeli pe pajeste, o paj nashavda lendar.

Athoska varegachi zumadipengo iklilo phurano manush andaro dorjaveste.

O manush mothoda: "Romana, na trubuj te aves ichardegodjaki thaj pherdeilehki odolese so si khamni. O Devel dija tuche e voshtako shingalo savo dzal te cherel buchi sar o chacho manush."

Romanache pharipe sasa baro, numaj voj nashti te paruvel gova situacija. Voj djela tar chereste thaj anda cikni Richini pe gova them. Sar Richini bajrovda gadija Romana dija lache chacho kamipe, thaj sikljovla las e chavoreske, bashaldeske chelipe thaj avere dzanglimata.

Von avile but pindzarde thaj cherde but love pala lacho dzuvdipe.

Romana thaj Richini hi- len majpashuni familija dziko

adjive thaj von san but pindzarde ando themeste sar njamo
Ursari.

Romana,
the Girl Who Founded
the Bear Clan

Once upon a time, there lived a beautiful Romani girl called Romana. She was so divinely beautiful that nobody could believe she was mortal. Romana charmed everyone – adults, children, animals and birds – not only because of her beauty, but also because of her kindness and innocence.

But, one day the impossible happened. Romana, a virgin who had never even kissed a man, discovered that she was pregnant. This caused her family great shame, so in her disgrace and desperation, Romana went to the river to drown herself. When she arrived at the bank of the river to jump in, however, the water receded from the bank. This surprised her, and she felt very scared. She tried again and again to jump into the water, but every time she tried, the water receded and she fell upon the riverbed. After many such attempts, she saw an old man appear from the river. He said to her, "Romana, do not feel ashamed or frightened. You are going to give birth to an animal that will be able to work like a man."

Romana despaired, but she listened to the man speaking. She resigned herself to her fate, returned home, and later gave birth to a bear cub. But as the cub began to grow, Romana fell more and more in love with it. She named it Richini. She taught Richini how to play games with the children and how to perform amusing tricks. Soon, Romana and her performing bear became very well known throughout the country, and they were able to earn a lot of money. Their lives were very comfortable thereafter, thanks to Richini's performances. Romana and Richini then became the founders of the clan of Roma called Ursari, a clan still traveling today with their performing bears. They are called the Bear Trainers.

Chemane

Lungo vakto nakhada kana ando vosheste dzivela Rromani chej Rubina e dadesa, i dejasa thaj e shtar phralenca.

Sako djive Rubina djeli ando vosheste. Jekh djive voj dikhla shukar manush savo cherda buchi sar o voshesko manush. Rubina pherda ando kamipeste. Numaj, voshesko manush na dzangla pala lako kamipe, thaj na dija sema pala Rubinako pherdo ilo. Voj mangla numaj lengo dikhipe, ali vosehesko manush naj seha leh jakha thaj ilo pala Rubina.

Rubina na dzangla so te cherel thaj phirda te dikhel dilo demono. O demono vacharda kaj vov shaj te locharel lache ako voj del leske piri familija. Bijakheski e kamipestar Rubina cherda sar demono mangla. O dilo, bilacho demono cherda lako dad ande chemane, laki dej ando jarko (gudalo), thaj lake shtar phrala ande shtar bricha (chemanache zhicurja).

Athoska varegachi sahatura Rubina achili korkori pe themeste. Naj seha- la laki familija, numaj chemane. Voj lela e chemane thaj astarda te bashalel. Lako bashalipe sasa but shukar, sar o kamipe, sar o pherdipe, sar o mothodipe. Rubinako mothodipe e chemanensa sasa sar lako dzuvdipe, baro pharipe pala familija. Lako bashalipe thaj djilavipe phande sasto vosh. Sar voj o vosh phanda, gadija phanda e voshesko manush.

Rubina thaj voshesko manush avile ando kamipeste. Rubina astarda te bashalel thaj djilabel baxtale, sige djila thaj chelipa. Voj bistarda pala piri familija. Akana pala Rubina kote sasa numaj voshesko manush thaj chemane. Numaj, na lungo!

O bilacho demono avilo jakhaldo pala gova baxtalipe thaj kamipe. Vov lelo pesa Rubina thaj lako manush ando deleste. Odolese so sigo mukla e phuv thaj vosh, o demono bistarda e chemane. E chemane achile bistarde thaj mukline ando vosheste dziko. . .

Jekh djive chororo chavo Lolo arakha e chemane. Ando momento kana Lolo lelo e chemane ande vasta, Lolo sasa phando. Vareso bandjavno djelo ando leste. Vov astarda te djilabel thaj bashavel pale gasave bashalipa thaj djila sar Rubina. Numaj, mora te dzanen, Lolo nikana na dzangla te bashavel vareso instrumento. Thoska, vov avilo baro chemanako virtuozo, thaj adjive lenge chavore san but pindzarde sar Rromano Chemanako njamo.

The Violin

A long time ago, Rubina, a beautiful Romani girl, lived in a forest with her parents and her four brothers. Every day, Rubina would go for walks in the forest. One day, she saw a handsome forest man and fell in love with him, though her love was unrequited. Though she loved him, the forest man refused to pay attention to Rubina, and this broke her heart. She tried in many different ways to make him pay attention to her, but nothing could persuade the man of her dreams to notice her. In her desperation, she approached a demon and begged for his help.

The demon promised to help her, but only if she would promise in return to surrender her parents and her brothers to the demon. She agreed to his request.

The demon took Rubina's four brothers and made of them four violin strings. Then, the demon built a violin out of her father. Finally, he used her mother to form the violin's bow. After a few hours, Rubina felt lonely, and she regretted her bargain. There was nobody left from her family. She had only the violin.

Rubina took the violin and started to play it. She played lovely, sorrowful music. Her music bewitched all the inhabitants and animals of the forest as well as the forest man himself. He then fell in love with Rubina, at long last. Rubina was elated that her love was requited now, and so she started to play happy music, music with spirit and joy. By the charms of her music, and by the good fortune of love, she forgot all about her sorrow for her family. For her, there were only the violin and the forest man. But, this would not last: for the demon envied their luck and happiness. He carried off Rubina and her lover to purgatory! But, in his anger, the demon forgot to bring the violin.

The violin then remained lost until Lolo, a Romani orphan, found it. The violin was magic, of course, and when Lolo took it in his hands, it bewitched him instantly. Something like a light entered into his body. He started to play the violin, the same music Rubina had played and just as beautifully, even though he had never played any instrument before that moment.

Lolo became a virtuoso violinist and his descendents have become very well known as the Romani violinist clan.

Sar Rroma Avile Bashalavne thaj Djilavne

Angla dur vakto dzivisarde o Rrom Ramiz thaj i Rromni Raba. Von avile but chorore thaj bokhale, thaj astarde te bandjaven thaj rudjaven e Devlese pala o baxt thaj lacho dzuvdipe. Von bandjavile talo jekh pajehko kash. Ramiz thaj Raba bandjavile sar dile pe sasto djive but bershengo, dziko jekh djive pajehko kash astarda te vacharel.

Pajehko kash dija vorba kaj von trubuj te len e Devlesko turvinjipe, thaj te cheren chemane e pajehko kashestar. Thaj, pajehko kash vacharda lendje: "O Devel mangel te del tuche baro muzikako, bashaldesko talento thaj barvalo dzuvdipe. Cher mandar lache chemane." Ramiz thaj Raba lundjarde gova turvinjipe thaj tradicija krzo lenge chavore, thaj sasti familija ikljarda sar baro Bashaldesko thaj Djilabesko njamo.

Ando gova vakto, e Thagareski Dur Gureski chej sasa nasvali thaj Thagar nashti te rodel vareko drab pala las. O Thagar ashundilo pala Bashaldesko thaj Djilabesko njamo, thaj mothoda e karnalende te idjaren len ando dvorco.

Kana Thagareski chej ashundja Rromano bashalipe voj sastivel. Odolese, baxtalo Thagar dija e Rromende e phuv thaj semunca pala chuvipe.

Thoska varegachi brshengo, kote, ande gova them, sasa bokhalo brsh. Sa dzuvdo sasa bokhalo. Rroma halisarde e sasto djiv. Kana von hale sa semunca, naj seha-leh khanchi pala hape. Numaj bokhalipe.

Thagar Dur Gur na mangla te dzanel pala gova bokhalipe thaj na mangla te hacharel gova baro problemo. Vov avilo sar sajekh, but armadino thaj roda o djiv e manushendar. Vov mothoda kaj sako manush trubuj te anel jekh trasta e djivesko, a kon naj leh, musaj te meren. Kote astarda mulesko daravipe.

Terno Rrom Ramche, Ramizesko thaj Rabako chavo, ashunda e dadesko turvinjipe.

Ramche djelo pe sako chirengo nurushoj thaj chidilo senunca dziko leski trasta sasa pherdi. Thagar seha-leh e bare jakha kana Ramche idjarda gova trasta.

Akana, Thagar seha-leh hape ando dvorco thaj vov mukla terno Ramche te dzuvdel.

Odolese, amaro Bashalavno thaj Djilavno njamo dzuvdel dziko adjive.

How the Roma Became Musicians and Singers

Once upon a time, there lived a very poor Romani couple, Ramiz and Raba. Because of their poverty, they decided to pray to God under a willow tree. They prayed very sincerely, and the willow tree began to speak to them. The tree told them that they should take God's advice and make a violin from the branches of the willow tree. When this was accomplished, the tree told them, God would give them a great musical talent and they would enjoy a comfortable life with music.

Ramiz and Raba followed this advice, and over time, through the generations, they became a large clan of musicians and singers.

One day, the daughter of the Emperor, Dur Gur, fell terribly ill. The Emperor was unable to find any medicine that could cure her. The Emperor had heard of the Romani musician clan, and so he ordered his servants to find them and bring them to the palace.

When the Emperor's daughter listened to the Romani music, she recovered. Out of gratitude, the Emperor gave the Roma a large plot of land and crops to plant.

After a few years, there was a famine in the land. All the people grew hungry, and the Roma were forced to eat all their stores of wheat. When all their crops were gone, they had nothing left to eat. But the Emperor still demanded his bag of wheat from the house of every family who farmed in his country. This was because he, too, had no food. He told the people that anybody who did not bring him the required bag of wheat would be killed.

Nobody had any wheat to bring him except Ramche, a

young Romani and a son of Ramiz and Raba. Ramche's father gave him some advice, and by taking it, he brought his family good fortune. On his father's advice, Ramche went to all the anthills and collected a few grains of wheat from each one until he had a full bag of wheat. The Emperor was surprised to get this bag of wheat, but he rewarded the young man's efforts by sparing the Roma. They were all allowed to live.

In time, through the generations, the clan grew and prospered. They remain a clan of good musicians and singers to this day.

Buka (Zalaga) Marno

Angla dur vakto kana sasa bokhalipe, nasvalipe, thaj kana
o shil halo sa dzuvdo pe phuvjate, but manusha mule e kali
bibijatar. Manusha nashade jekh averestar. Von na mangle
te azhutinen jekh averestar ande pharipeste thaj nasvalipeste.
Nasvalipe sasa pale, sar pala chorore gadija pala barvale, thaj
khonik naj seha-leh e Devlesko akharipe.

Devel e melalengo, Melalo, thaj Devel e nasvalipengo, Nasvalo, dikhle pala gova thaj hasajvile pala manusheske problemura thaj doshalipa. Lachi, Devel e lachendar, zumavili te
azhutinel e manushende thaj rodel o godjaverno drom pala
gova. Voj vacharili e Nasvalensa thaj Melalensa: ako vareko
manush azhutinel te del buka marno pala bokhale, thaj so-
vipe prdal pe racha pala bikherenge, gadija manush mora te
dzuvdel thaj sastardivel. Melalo thaj Nasvalo na pachavdje
ando gova shajipe, thaj Nasvalo manglo te dzal e Lachesa
te hasajven pala piro phagaripe. Nasvalo cherdol pes ando
bakroro thaj djelo e Lachesa pe phuvesko drom.

E kali bibija, bokhalipe, xoljardipe thaj mulipe bajrovili
maskaro manushende. Lachi thaj Nasvalo djele katar o udar
dziko udar, rode zalaga marno thaj khonik na mangla te
putarel udara. Khonik na mangla te del vorba lasa. Ando
treno kana vareko na mangla te putaren o udar Nasvalo
phurda mulipeski hava ando lesko cher. But manusha thaj
chavore mule. Lachi thaj Nasvalo djele krzo but forende thaj
gavende numaj khonik na azhutinel lendje. Nasvalo hasajvilo.

Von djele, djele thaj avile dziko jekh buhljipe.

Andothan, Lachi dikhla jekh chajralo uchipe- burdelji.
Gova sasa phurani cher, pala gova vakto bishajipe. Gova
avile vareke save san but chorore deso sa chorore manusha.
Gova avile vareke save san but mudarde deso sa mudarde

71

manusha. Gova sasa manushesko cher. Voj avili dziko burdeljesko udar thaj ashunda vareko manushesko chib savo voj na pindzarda. Andothan, Lachi phenda: "Azhutinen man, lache manushalen! Bokhali sem, dema jekh zalaga marno, ka merav e bokhalipestar!"

Sigo, o udar sasa putarda, thaj pe udareste avilo Mehmed -cherehko shorutno. Vov phenda: "Hi-man cira marno pala tute. Ach, ka anav cira. Ako na dares e nasvalipestar av andre, lachi dzuvli! Me chavore ka meren e kali bibijatar."

Lachi dija andre ando burdeljeste, thaj dikhla shov chavore kaj sutle pasha e jagate. Kate avili lendje dej, savi rudjisarda e Devleske thaj rovlja. Pasha late beshla nasvalo dzukel. Mehmed anda cira marno, thaj ulada marno ando deshojekh pale kotora. Pale savore jekh zalaga marno. Vov na bistarda o bakroro thaj o dzukel. Mehmed thovda pire chavore pe jekh rigate thaj cherda o than pala Lachi thaj lako bakroro.

"Savo lachoilehko manush," gndisarda Lachi, "vov thaj lenge familija musaj te achen dzuvinde. Mehmed trubuj te arakhel manushesko njamo ande phuvjate. Vov si lacho manush."

Kana nasvali familija sutla, Lachi phurda o sastipe thaj baxtalipe ando burdeljeste. Voj muklja but hape thaj pipe pala Mehmedake familija, thaj pasha e jageste, pherdo e sumnakajengo, duruvlji.

Kataro gova vakto Lachi si sajekh e Mehmedake familijasa.

A Bite of Bread

There was a time, a long time ago, when people were full of hate and refused to help one another. Because of this, their lives were full of cold, starvation, and illness; and the plague killed a great many people. The God of dirt, Melalo, and the God of illness, Nasvalo, laughed at the misery of the people and enjoyed watching them suffer in their misfortune.

Nobody was safe from illness, and certainly nobody received any compassion from Melalo and Nasvalo, until the Goddess of Good, named Lachi, decided to outwit these two evil Gods. She decided to protect life on Earth.

Lachi tried to spare, if not everybody, then at least those who had shown themselves to be kind-hearted and helpful. Those, at least, would bring hope to future generations of humanity.

After considering her plan carefully, she asked Melalo and Nasvalo for just one favor. She would undertake a mission to Earth where she would appear before the people, family by family, and ask them for help. Those who offered to help her, to give her just a bite of bread and hospitality during the cold and hungry nights, would in turn enjoy her own good protection from the misery brought by the wicked gods. Melalo and Nasvalo did not believe that Lachi's plan would be successful. But, as they wanted to gloat over her failure, they suggested that Nasvalo should go with Lachi to witness her humility. Nasvalo disguised himself: he took the form of a lamb and went with Lachi on her mission of mercy.

When they arrived on Earth, they found nothing but misery: the plague was spreading, people were more unkind to one another than ever, and all the people had to look forward to was death.

Lachi and Nasvalo went from door to door, then, asking each household to spare a little bite of bread. But, nobody opened the door. When it became clear that a household would not help them, Nasvalo blew his breath upon the house, killing everybody inside. Because nobody wanted to speak to Lachi, because nobody spared her just a bite of bread, people all over the world were dying.

When Lachi and Nasvalo had almost completed their mission on Earth, Nasvalo was sure of his victory. They had gone through many cities and villages, leaving death and emptiness in their wake. Finally, they came to a clearing and saw a small cave inside a grass-covered hill.

"This is an odd way to live," thought Lachi. Lachi realized that whoever lived in this cave must be the poorest of families on Earth, even more hated and shunned than the others they had met. Lachi came close to the cave and put her ear to the grassy entrance. The cave was certainly somebody's home, since she heard human voices inside speaking a language that was strange to her. Outside, it was cold and the night was coming very fast.

She called for help as she approached the entrance of the cave. Nasvalo, still disguised as a lamb, came with her. She called out, "Help, good people, could you give me just a bite of bread? I am going to die from hunger!"

The grass entrance opened suddenly, and Mehmed, the host, put his head outside. He said to the woman and her lamb, "Good woman, stay if you are not scared of plague and death. My children are dying, but I do have some bread to share with you. But one moment and I will bring it for you."

Mehmed went back into the cave, and Lachi did not wait outside. She, too, entered the cave to see this man's family for herself. Mehmed, the good-hearted man, was surprised that the strange woman at his cave door did not fear their illness. He invited her to bring her lamb inside, too, because of the cold of night.

Lachi saw six children sleeping around a very poor fire, and all of them had the plague. They were dying very quietly.

Their mother sat in the corner of the cave, crossing her hands, crying and praying to God. A dog was lying near the mother. Mehmed made a place near the fire for Lachi and her lamb after rearranging the children. Then, he brought a small piece of bread and divided it into eleven equal morsels. He had even provided pieces of bread for the dog and the lamb.

"Good-hearted man, this Mehmed," thought Lachi to herself. "He and his family should survive this terrible time on Earth. Mehmed should become the protector of humanity on Earth."

Later that night, when everyone slept deeply, Lachi blew her breath into the cave, and instead of misery there was goodness for the family. The six children, their mother, the dog and the host, Mehmed, immediately became healthy and well.

Early in the morning, while the healthy family was still asleep, Lachi left behind a barrel of gold and great quantities of nourishing food. Then, she and Nasvalo departed, leaving the Earth. She had succeeded in her mission to protect humanity and preserve goodness.

Since that day, too, she has always looked after the descendants of the good-hearted Mehmed.

Dipe Alav

Ando dumutnipeste, kote dzivela baxtali familija: i dej, o dad thaj lenge murshikano chavo. Chavo seha-leh pandz brshengo kana gova baxtalipe chinda dejako mulipe, thaj kana chavoresko dad nasvajlilo. Khonik na mangla te azhutinel lendje odolese so seha-len kalo muj thaj odolese so avile nasvale thaj chorore. But brshengo cikno chavo azhucharda e dadese. Lengo dzuvdipe sasa pharo, but pharo dziko...

Jekh teharin o dad vazdinjalo e dozacharipesa thaj vacharda e chavese:

"Akana si terno manush, naj si cikno chavo. Av kote pasha mande, Dervish. Me mangav vareso te vacharav tuche. Ando suno me dikhlem phakali Luludji. Voj mothoda, kaj tu Dervish, mo chavo, trubul te rodes bendjalo praxo thaj baxtalo sahato. Gova trubul te azhutinel man thaj shaj te sastivav. Numaj, tu trubul te dzas pe dromeste. Pe gova dromeste, rudjav tut, na dikh pe stingo rig, na dikh pe chacho rig, na dzal pale. Dza chacho, thaj dikh angla pes. Na bistar, musaj te aves pachavno, thaj ako das alav pala vareso, musaj te aches phando pala gova alav."

Dervish djelo pe dromeste. Kana avilo dziko baro paj, kote naj seha vareso phurd, naj seha vareso pajehko. Numaj, Dervish musaj te dikhel angla pes. Ando treno kana vov gndisarda so te cherel, ashunda o krlo andare pajestar:

"Me sem macho. Nasvalo sem. Me dzanav kaj dzas thaj sose dzas pe dromeste. Me ka azhutinav tuche dziko avere rigate ako das alav. Kana rodes bendjalo praxo, dema cira mandje."

Dervish dija alav. Ando momento kote sasa phurdo prdal pe sasto baro paj. Dervish phirda dziko avere rigate.

77

Pe avere rigate kote sasa dvorco. Trushalo Dervish phuchlja e Thagar pala jekh taxtaj paj te pijel, numaj Thagar mothoda:

"Me dzanav kaj thaj sose dzas pe dromeste. Ka dav tuche o paj te pijes ako das alav; kana rodes bendjalo praxo dema cira mandje. Mo ambrol nashti te del bijanipe but brshengo."

Dervish dija alav, pilo paj, thaj djelo durder pe dromeste. Vov djelo, djelo krzo jekh bari xalimata thaj avilo dziko aver dvorco. Kate naj seha vareko dzuvdipesko semno. Sa sasa sar muklino. Vov djelo opashin thaj. . .

Dervish dikhla shukar princeza. Princeza sasa phandi. Kote, pasha las, sovda jekh phakavno sap (zmajo). Polohko, biashundo, Dervish mukla las andaro kavezo. Princeza dija leske bendjalo praxo, thaj vov dija lache alav te ka ansurelhe lakeo,lkana vov godjaverelv las.

Voj mothoda leske sa e phakalese sapese. Ako Dervish thovel cira bendjalo praxo pe leste, phakalo sap ka cherdivel ando baxtalo sahato. Bendjalo praxo thaj baxtalo sahato shaj te cheren but sastipe thaj baxtalipe. Thaj Dervish cherda gova. Vov thovda cira praxo pe phakalo sap, thaj o sapo sasa cherdino ando baxtalo sahato. Dervish sigo lelo o sahato thaj aver praxo, thaj nashadilo e pirese dadese.

Pale, vov djelo prdal pe xalimata, thaj avilo dziko Thagaresko dvorco. Dervish thovda cira praxo thaj baxtalo sahato pe ambroleste. Ando treno kate avile but bare ambrolenge. O Thagar dija leske duruvlji, thaj ande duruvljate but sumnakaj thaj dukati, thaj jekh sumnakuni vordon e duj grastenca.

Dervish djelo, djelo thaj avilo dziko baro paj. Kana dikhla o macho, dija e machese cira bendjalo praxo thaj thovda pe lestar baxtalo sahato. Ando treno macho sasa sasto thaj cherda pale baro phurdo pala Dervish. Dervish phirda dziko avere rigate. Pe avere rigate azhucharda les baro pajalo barvalipe e but sumnakajenca. Macho dija leske gova dipe.

Ande agoreski minuta Dervish avilo chere. Vov dija dadese bendjalo praxo thaj thovda pe lesko chikat baxtalo sahato. Ando treno o dad sasa sasto thaj baxtalo, thaj vazdindja pe prnenge.

Dervish thaj lesko dad, djele pe dromeste: prdal pe paj,

prdal pe xalipe. Kote, pe aver rigate, azhucharda shukar princeza.

Ako das alav, musaj te aches phando e alavesa.

Savore dzivisarde ande sastipe thaj baxtalipe but brshengo athoska. . .

Promise

Once upon a time, there lived a happy family: a mother, a father, and their son. Their happiness was shattered, however, by the time their son turned five years old when the mother died. Around the same time, the boy's father took very ill. Nobody wanted to help the boy and his father because of their dark skin, their illness, and their poverty. So the small boy took care of his sick father for many years, and they endured a very hard life.

One morning, the boy's father awoke in a happy mood and called his son to him. "Come, Dervish, and sit on my bed. I want to tell you something. You are no longer a small boy. You have grown into a young man. I dreamed last night of a nymph. Her name was Luludji. She told me that if my son could find some magic dust and a lucky watch, I would recover from my illness and we would be lucky for the rest of our lives. But, my son, the journey to find this dust and watch is a mysterious one. On this journey, you must neither turn left nor turn right; and nor can you go backwards. Son, you must go only straight ahead. And one final thing: you must always keep your word. You must be honest with everyone you meet."

So, to help his father, Dervish set out on this quest. First, he came to a wide lake. He knew he could not turn left or right or go backwards, so he must move straight across it. But, there was no bridge over the lake, and the boy had neither a boat nor anyone to help him get across.

As the boy thought about his problem, he heard a voice from the lake. The voice spoke, "I am a fish. I am sorrowful and very sick. I know the reason for your quest, young man, and I will help you cross the lake if you promise me something.

80

If you find the magic dust for your father, sprinkle a little of it on my scales."

Dervish promised the fish he would do so. Suddenly, a bridge spanning the lake appeared before his eyes. He crossed the lake easily, and he continued his journey until he came to a castle.

In the castle, Dervish asked the Emperor for a glass of water. The Emperor replied, "I know about your quest, young man. I will give you a glass of water if you promise to give me a little bit of the magic dust. My pear tree hasn't produced any pears for years."

Dervish made his promise to the Emperor, and he was grateful for the glass of water. Continuing along his way, Dervish traversed a long desert until he reached another castle. There was no sign that anyone lived in this castle. Everything seemed to be abandoned.

While Dervish walked around, he suddenly saw a beautiful princess in a cage. She had been captured by a dragon. He rescued the princess from the cage and, out of gratitude, she gave him the magic dust he sought. She then asked him to come back and marry her after he had finished his journey.

Dervish promised her that he would do so. The princess explained to him that the dragon was presently sleeping. If he spilled a little of the magic dust on the dragon, it would be transformed into a lucky watch. She told him that the magic dust he carried would be more powerful if he also possessed the lucky watch. So, Dervish did exactly what she told him to do. He spilled a little of the magic dust on the dragon, and as she had promised, the dragon changed into the lucky watch. Dervish took the watch and the magic dust and began his journey back to his father.

He went back through the desert and came to the Emperor's castle. He spilled a little of the magic dust on the pear tree and touched it with the lucky watch. In an instant, large, delicious pears appeared on the tree. Because of this, the Emperor gave Dervish a barrel of gold ducats and a golden carriage with two beautiful horses. Dervish then continued his journey back to his father. Arriving at the lake, he sprinkled the fish with magic dust and touched its scales with the lucky watch. In a flash, the fish became healthy and Dervish saw another bridge appear to take him home. He crossed to the other side where he found a pleasant surprise. The fish had given him wealth from the depths of the lake.

Dervish finally returned home. He gave the magic dust to his father and touched his head with the lucky watch. At that moment, his father was cured. His father rose to his feet, healthy and happy.

Then, they journeyed together to the castle where the beautiful princess was waiting. Dervish kept his promise to the princess and they were married. The three of them then lived happily ever after in health and contentment.

Dilo

Jekhethane dzivina trin phrala: duj godjaverne thaj jekh dilo. Duj godjaverne, Yanko thaj Djelem, cherde buchi pe sasto djive ande vosheste thaj ande umalinate, dziko dilo pe akhardipe Dilo cherda but problemura. Duj godjaverne cherde o plano te nashaven Dilo avri e cherestar, thaj thovde les ande shtala. Sar gndisarde gadija cherde.

Yanko thaj Djelem mothodile e Dilese kataro gova plano, thaj sa gurumne thaj bakre thovde pe umalinate. Plano sasa, kana von akharde gurumne thaj bakre pe anaveste, save pashaven lendje, trubuj te achen lenca. Dilo akharda leski gurumni Mura, thaj numaj voj achili lesa. Avere gurumne thaj bakre achile e phralenca.

Kana perda o rach, Dilo dija e gurumnache o khas te xal thaj mothoda: "Me ka icharav memelin tuche dziko tu xas, thaj athoska tu mandje." Gurumni Mura xala, xala, thaj Dilo icharda memelin lungo vakto. Kana voj gatisarda, perda te sovel. Dilo sasa odjalo thaj bokhalo. Vov mangla i gurumni te vazdel, numaj gurumni sar saki gurumni, cherda so mangel. Akana Dilo lelo o churik thaj chinda las, uzharda leski morchi, chinda lesko sasto prno, thaj djelo ando gaveste.

Vov akharda but dzukele thaj thovda lendje e gurumnache prno te xan. Athoska vacharda: "Ashun man, dzukele. Me ka avav ando parashtuj pala love, trubuj te pochinen mas." Numaj dzukele sar dzukele, xale thaj mirisarde.

Dilo djelo chere. Vov lelo muklino mas thaj morchi thaj djelo ande plajinate te bichinel gova.

Bahval zuralo phurda, a Lolo avilo ande plajinache vosh-este. Patrina civisarde. Bahval sasa but zuralo, thaj krange phagarde pe phuvjate. Ando treno kana Lolo phiravda talo jekh kasheste, jekh krango phagarda thaj mudarda les, a dujto krango lelo leski pherdi trasta, opre, vucho pe kasheste. Dilo mothoda: "Lacho! Tumen pochinde o mas. Me ka avav tehara pala love."

Vov djelo chere pale thaj mothoda phralende so sasa, thaj sar bichinda o mas. Leske phrala garadino xasajvile.

Teharinaha, Dilo djelo ande plajinate te rodel love pala mas. Vov arakhlo talo e kasheste thaj mothoda: "Dema love. Me bichinavlem tumen o mas." Numaj kash sar o kash. Na dija vorba. "Me chinav tut. Ashunes man? Ako na das o love, ka chinav tut." Dilo sasa ratvalo.

Vov lelo leski chindali thaj chinda o kash. Ando treno kana o kash perda pe phuvjate, kote ande xava sasa bendjalo praxo savo andrel ando Dilo. Talo kasheste sasa sumnakaj ande duruvljate. Dilo mothoda: "Shukar. E daravipestar musaj te pochinen. Gova si o drom sar varese pochinen love kana ande lendje kokale andrel daravipe." Vov lelo e duruvlji e sumnakajenca, thaj ando treno vareko krlo phenda: "Me sem bendjalo praxo thaj akana ka avav tusa sajekh."

Vov djelo chere. Kana leske phrala dikhle sumnakaj von mangle te choren lestar.

"Vov si dilo. Nashti te dzanel thaj dikhel ako amen choren," mothodile phrala.

Dilo irisarda sigo:

"Manusha ande vosheste mangen but mas. Von phuchle man pala but, but mas. Von mangen te pochinen desh duruvlja."

Yanko thaj Djelem chinade sa gurumna thaj bakra. Von thovde o mas pe vordoneste thaj djele ande plajinate.

Von djele but djivengo te roden e manusha save trubul te pochinen o mas.

Jekhetane djele dur ande vosheste thaj dikhle but ruva opashin. E daravipestar Yanko thaj Djelem nashadile. Ruva xale sasto mas. Duj godjaverne phrala naj seha-len sumnakaj thaj dukati, numaj nango dzuvdipe.

Dilo

Once, there were three brothers. Two of them were clever, but one was foolish. The two clever brothers, Yanko and Djelem, worked in the forests and in the fields all day long. But the foolish brother, Dilo, only wasted his time and caused problems for other people in the village. Dilo was a constant embarassment to Yanko and Djelem.

The two clever brothers devised a plan to get Dilo out of their house. Yanko and Djelem called Dilo to them, and they told him they were going to move him out of the house and into the stable. Next, in order to divide their livestock, they put all the cattle out to pasture and then called each creature by name: whoever the cattle came to, he should keep it as his own. So, Dilo called his cow, Mura, and she came to him; no others came to Dilo. Therefore, all the other cattle belonged to the two clever brothers. Dilo shared his stable stall with his cow, Mura.

When night came, Dilo brought some hay to his cow. He said to her, "I am going to help you. I will hold the lantern while you eat the hay from my hand. When you are done, you must hold the lantern for me while I eat."

Mura began eating the hay and for a while, Dilo was patient. When she had eaten all her hay, she fell into a deep sleep. Dilo was hungry and angry. He tried to wake his cow, but Mura, being a cow, was not inclined to help him.

Angered that the cow would not hold the lantern for him, Dilo took his knife and slaughtered her. He removed her hide, cut off her legs, put the four legs over his shoulder, and then went into the village. He called four dogs and gave each of them a cow's leg to eat. Then he told them, "Alright, dogs. You took the cow's legs, and they are now sold to you. I will come tomorrow to collect the money that you owe me for them." But the dogs, being dogs, were busy eating and growling.

Dilo went home, took the rest of the beef and cowhide, and then walked up the mountain to sell it. A strong wind was blowing. When Dilo had reached the interior of the mountain forest, the wind became more and more powerful. Leaves were rustling and branches started to break and fall down. Just as Dilo reached the base of a tall tree, a branch broke off and fell on his shoulder. At the same time, another branch tore away his meat sack and thrust it into the tree.

Dilo addressed the tree. "Alright. You took my meat. It is now sold to you. I will come tomorrow to collect the money that you owe me for it."

Dilo came home and told his brothers all that had happened and how he had sold the meat. His brothers congratulated him, with irony. The following morning Dilo went to get the money for the meat he had sold. First he went to the tree on the mountain and said, "I have come to collect the money you owe me for the cow's meat." But the tree, being only a tree, was silent.

"I will cut you down," Dilo said angrily. "Do you hear me? I am going to cut you down if you refuse to pay the money to me."

The tree remained silent and Dilo became furious. He took his axe and cut down the tree. As the tree began to fall, magic dust appeared in the air and began to settle on Dilo. When the tree crashed to earth, Dilo saw a barrel of gold at the uprooted end. He declared, "Good! This is fine payment indeed. You must have been very scared of me."

He claimed the gold-filled barrel, and at that moment a haunting voice said to him, "I am the magic dust that penetrated your body. I will help you and be with you for the rest of your life." Satisfied, Dilo went home with the barrel of gold. When his brothers saw it, they wanted to steal it.

"Dilo is a fool," they said. "He would not notice if we stole the barrel for ourselves."

Dilo overheard his brothers speaking, and he immediately devised a tricky plan. Dilo said to the brothers, "The people on the mountain who bought my meat, they need a lot more of it. They asked me to bring more meat, and they promised ten more barrels like this one to pay for it."

Yanko and Djelem became greedy, and they slaughtered all their cattle. Then they loaded all the meat onto a wagon and drove up the mountain. For a long time Yanko and Djelem looked for customers, but of course, as Dilo secretly knew, there were none.

At last a pack of hungry wolves appeared, but instead of eating Yanko and Djelem, they ate all the meat in the wagon. The two clever brothers did not get any barrels of gold, but they did at least escape with their lives.

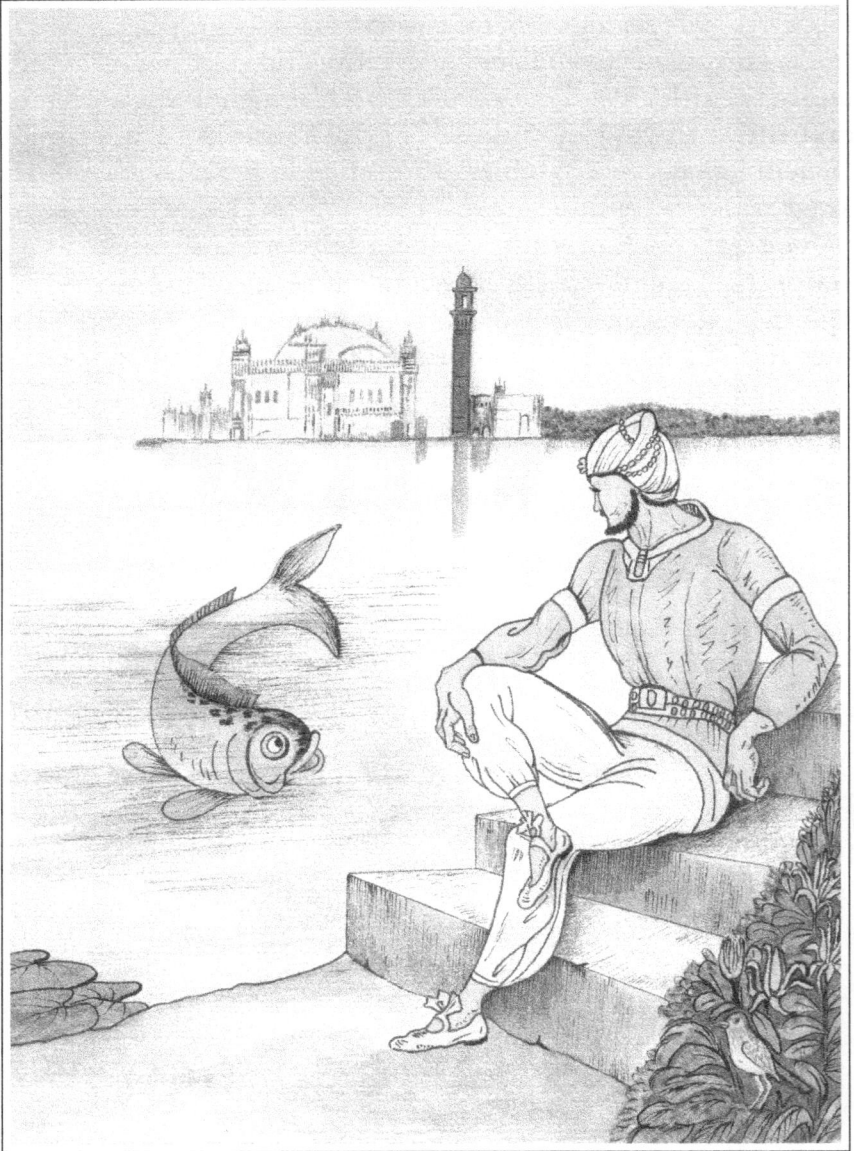

Macho

Palal efta voshtengo thaj efta pajengo dzivisarde o Thagar Manush thaj leski Rromni Thagarica Papusha. Voj avili nasvali e pherde ilestar. Pharipe vulisarda leski odji. Voj mangla o chavo, numaj gova sasa bishajipe pala las. Odolese, Thagarica Papusha achili but brshengo ande pataveste. Thagar Manush rovlja thaj garada jasva e manushendar uzo baroro paj, kaj khonik nashti te dikhel lesko bizuralipe.

Jekh drom, kana vov beshla uzo baroro paj, leske cherchale jasva pherde ando pajeste. Ando treno kote avilo but bojavengo macho. Thagar sasa daravdo, a majbut kana macho astarda te vacharel:

"Kamlo Thagar Manush, me ka azhutinav tuche. Le man tusa ando dvorco, thaj phend e Rromnjache kaj trubuj te cherel man pala o hape. Voj trubul te cherel man numaj pe dromeste sar me dzav te mothovav tuche akana.

Angluno, voj mora te chinel mo por. Dujto, voj mora te shulavel mrne krljushti thaj den len pala e grasni te xan. Trito, Thagarica Papusha mora te del e dzukelese mrni drobovina. Shtarto, voj mora te thovel ando boshtinako phuvjate duj bare kokala. Pe agoreste, voj musaj te xal man. Le man chere, thaj ka dikhes. Me mangav te azhutinav tuche. Me dav mo alav."

Thagar Manush lelo macho thaj djelo chere. Kana avilo chere vov mothoda e thagaricache so sasa thaj so musaj te cheren.

Thaj, von astarde e buchasa. Von cherde sar macho phenda: krljushti xala i grasni, dzukela xala drobovina, kokale thovda ande phuv, thaj voj korkori xala macho.

Kana grasni xala krljushti, voj khamnisajvel, e drobovinatar dzukela khamnisajvel. E duj kokalendar andare phuvjate astarde te bajroven duj bare xarna, thaj e machestar

Thagarica Papusha khamnjisarda.

Athoska, grasni bijanda duj khurora, dzukela duj cikne dzukele, phuv duj xarna, thaj Thagarica Papusha bijanda duj murshikane chavore, Chiriklo thaj Miriklo.

Pala deshoinja djivengo Chiriklo thaj Miriklo avile sar deshoinja brshenge. Duj phrala gndisarde te dzan pe dromeste opashin lumijate te pindzaren o them. Numaj ando gova vakto lengo dad o Thagar Manush mula. "Pherde ilehki Thagarica Papusha nashti te achel korkori ande dvorco," gndisarde duj phrala. Chiriklo thaj Miriklo ande o kris kaj Chiriklo trubul te dzal pe dromeste, dziko Miriklo musaj te achel e dejasa. Von djele ande boshtin; kote avile duj xarna, duj dzukela, thaj duj grasta. Pala sako phral jekh xarno jekh dzukela, jekh gras. Chiriklo phenda e Miriklese: "Ako hi-man vareso problemo, musaj te dikhes ando xarneste. Ako si xarno ratvalo, me sem ande bare probleme thaj me trubuj chiro azhutipe."

Chiriklo, lesko gras, thaj dzukela furnavile pe vazduho dziko chindile thaj trushale avile ando baro foro. Chiriklo mangla te pijen o paj, numaj kote naj seha o paj. Vov boldisarda pashe thaj dikhla phuri, bizhavni Rromni. Vov phuchla las trubul li vareko azhutipe. E barenca jakhenca voj dikhla les thaj phenda: "But vakto nakhada sar vareko phuchla trubul li vareko azhutipe kate." Voj cherda jekh bari bivorbaki pauza thaj phenda: "Gova si Pashesko foro. Kate si baro xajing thaj ande xajingate san trin phakavna sapa. Trin... Jekh hi-leh jekh shoro, dujto hi-leh duj shorengo, trito hi-leh trin shorengo. Sako brsh amen musaj te den jekh rakli pala len. Pala saki rakli hi-amen saranda djivengo paj ando foreste. Gova brsh Pasheski chej Sumnali musaj te dzal. Pasha xasarda i chej Terni ande plajinate, thaj ako xasarel gova chej, vov ka merel. Ande teharinako Sumnali musaj te avel uzo xajing kana phakavne sapa aven. Me dikhav bendjavno semno pe chiro chikateste. Tu shaj te azhutines amen. Dza pe xajingeste. Kana jekhshoresko phakavno sap iklovel te lel shukar Sumnali, chin lesko shoro. Thoska kana iklel dujshoresko phakavno sap, chin leske duj shora. Kana chines trinshoresko phakavno sap, na dara, ka avel brshind thaj andare xajing ka perel shudro, vuzho paj. Trubul te avel lacho pala savore."

Chiriklo djelo pe xajingate. Vov hacharda kaj sa trubul te avel lacho. Sa sasa sar bizhavni Romni mothoda. Kote avili shukar rakli. Voj rovlja thaj azhucharda pala piro mulipe. Chiriklo phenda e dzuklese te arakhel rakli, thaj vov achilo e grastesa te mudarel phakavne sapa. Chiriklo chinda jekhshoreko, thaj dujshoresko thaj trinshoresko phakavno sap.

Ando treno astarda brshind te perel thaj dzal vuzho paj andare xajingate. Shukar Sumnali, Chiriklo, gras thaj dzukela djele ando dvorco. Pasha sasa but baxtalo thaj pala Sumnali thaj Chiriklo cherda baro bijav.

Jekh rachako, vareso bendjalo sasa so vazdindja o Chiriklo andaro suno. Vov pashavda dziko pendzeri thaj dikhla bari jag ande plajinate. Sumnali mothoda kataro trin phakale save dzuvden ande plajinate. Voj mothoda leske kon dzal ande plajinate nikana na avel chere. Jekh drom lachi phen Terni nashavda ande plajinate odolese so na mangla te merel e phakavnendar sapendar, thaj nikana na irisarda chere.

Chiriklo djelo pe plajinate. Vov hacharda kaj shaj vareso te azhutinel. Kana Chiriklo avilo ande plajinate kote beshle trin phakale opashin jagate thaj opashin varesave bara. Von vacharde leske te beshel. Numaj, ko angluno, vov mora te del trin leske balorja kaj phakale shaj te phanglen lesko gras pe kasheste. Chiriklo dija trin balorja. Ando treno, phakale phurde ande balorja trin dromengo, thaj Chiriklo, gras thaj lesko dzukela cherde ando trin bare bara.

Dur dureske, chere beshlo Miriklo thaj kana dikhla o rat pe pireste xarneste, vov dzangla kaj Chiriklo hi - leh problemura. Vov lelo o gras, dzukel thaj xarno thaj djelo pe dromeste. Pala gasavo drom sasa pala Miriklo, thaj kana avilo trushalo thaj chindilo, avilo ando Pashesko foro. Kote sasa bizhavni, phuri Rromni savi mothodili sa so sasa. Voj mothodili e Miriklese ako phakale roden leske sheja jal balorja, vov na trubul te del. Gadija Miriklo djelo ande plajinate. Kana avilo kote beshle trin phakale opashin jagate thaj opashin e barende.

93

Von rode lestar trin balorja te phenden lesko gras, numaj Miriklo irisarda kaj hi-leh o lanco pala o gras. Vov mothoda dile paramicha, cherda dilimata pala lendje, thaj cherda len dziko mulikano xasavipe. Von mukle piri kontrala thaj Miriklo ispidarda lenge ande jagate. Ando treno phakalenge bendjalipa avile mukline thaj bara astarde te cheren aril. Varese avile vosha thaj varese manusha.

Kote avilo lesko phral: Chiriklo xasajvisarda, gras rimi-tardisarda, thaj dzukela basharisarda. Duj phrala pherde ande angalate. Numaj, kote avili shukar rakli thaj von dzan-gle kaj gova sasa Pasheski chej, Terni. Miriklo dikla Terni e bare jakhenca thaj Terni diklja Miriklo. Kote, ando ando angluno dikhipe, bijanda o kamipe. Jekhethane djele ando dvorco. Savore avile baxtale. Chiriklo thaj Sumnali achile ando Pashesko foreste, savo Pasha del lendje sar baro dipe. Pasha cherda o bijav pala Miriklo thaj Terni.

Athoska bijav von, Miriklo thaj Terni, djele chere kaj achili Thagarica Papusha. Thagarica Papusha nashti te avel korkori.

The Fish

Behind the seven forests and seven lakes lived handsome King Manush and his wife, Queen Papusha. But the queen grew more and more ill because of a deep, soulful sorrow. She was not able to have a child. This saddened her so much that she stayed in bed for a full year.

King Manush felt very sorry for his Queen. In secret, he would visit the lake so that nobody could see his weakness, and there he would cry bitterly.

Once, when he came to the lake, he sat down on the shore and his tears fell into the water. At that moment, a colourful fish appeared. This surprised King Manush, especially when the fish started to speak.

"Dear King Manush," the fish said. "I know your sorrow, and I will help you. Take me with you to your castle and tell your wife, Queen Papusha, that she should make a meal of me. The meal must be made, however, exactly in the way I am going to explain to you now."

The fish explained. "First, she should take a knife and cut open my stomach. Second, she should scrape off my scales to feed a mare from her feedbag. Third, she should give my intestines to your dog. Fourth, she should plant two of my big bones in the earth of your garden. Finally, she should eat me. Only take me home and do as I have instructed, and this will help Queen Papusha and you. I promise."

King Manush took the fish and went home. He explained to Queen Papusha what had happened and what the fish had told him she should do.

The Queen followed the instructions perfectly. In a short while, the mare who had eaten the scales became pregnant. The bitch who had eaten the intestines also became pregnant.

The two bones planted in the garden's earth grew up into sabres. And finally, after eating the fish, Queen Papusha became pregnant, too.

The mare foaled two colts; the bitch threw two puppies; and Queen Papusha gave birth to two sons, Chiriklo and Miriklo.

In nineteen days, the twin sons aged nineteen years. The two brothers were planning to take a trip around the world, then, but their father the King died. Because their mother, Queen Papusha, did not want to be left alone in her grief, Chiriklo and Miriklo decided that Chiriklo should go on the trip, and Miriklo should stay with his mother. Then, they went outside into the garden where they saw two sabres, two dogs and two horses, one for each son.

Chiriklo told Miriklo: "If I encounter trouble, you will know by looking at your sabre. If it is bloody, it means that I need your help."

Chiriklo and his horse then took flight and began their journey around the world. They stopped when they were exhausted, and they found themselves in a big city. Chiriklo wanted a drink of water, but there was no water to be found.

When Chiriklo looked around, he saw an old, wise woman sitting alone. He asked her if she needed any help. It had been a long time since anybody had asked her if she needed anything, and so she was surprised at Chiriklo's kindness. She said to him, "In the Pasha's city, there is a large well. In the well live three fierce dragons. One has one head, the second has two heads, and the third has three heads. Every year, we have to sacrifice a girl to the dragons, and after that they give us enough water only for forty days, and no longer. This year it is Sumnali's turn to be sacrificed, the Pasha's daughter. He lost his first daughter Terni at the nearby mountain, and if he loses his only remaining child, he will surely die. Early in the morning, Sumnali will be sacrificed to the dragons." She then looked closely at the young man, saying, "I see a magic sign on your forehead. You could help us. Please, go to the well. At the moment when the first dragon comes out to get the beautiful Sumnali, take your sabre and cut off his head. Then the two-headed dragon will come out of the well and after him the three-headed dragon. Cut off their heads as fast as you can. Do not be startled or afraid. As soon as you have cut off the dragons' heads, it will start to rain and the well will give us clear water. It will benefit all of us, here, not just Sumnali and her father."

So, Chiriklo went to the well. He believed that he could save the Pasha's city and his daughter. Everything happened, next, the way the old woman had described. There was a beautiful girl crying and waiting to be eaten by the dragons. Chiriklo told his dog to mind the girl so that nobody should come close to her. He mounted his horse, took his sabre and waited for the terrible dragons.

When the dragons emerged from the well, Chiriklo beheaded the one-headed dragon, then the two-headed dragon, and finally the three-headed dragon. Then, as it started to rain, clear water began to flow from the well.

Chiriklo retrieved the beautiful Sumnali and together, with his horse and dog, he brought her before the Pasha. The Pasha was the happiest man in the world, at that moment, and so he promised Sumnali's hand to Chiriklo. Both Chiriklo and Sumnali were happy, and they were soon married.

That night, something strange woke Chiriklo from a dream. He went to the window and saw a whole mountain on fire. Sumnali woke, too, and she explained to him what had happened to her sister.

Her sister Terni had gone to the mountain to escape being sacrificed to the dragons, and she had never returned. This was because of the three nymphs living on the mountain: whoever journeyed to the mountain never returned. Chiriklo decided to go and see what he could do to help find Sumnali's sister. He mounted his horse, took his dog, attached his sabre, and went to the mountain.

When he arrived, he found three nymphs sitting beside a fire surrounded by many stones. They asked him to join them, but, before he was allowed to, he ought first to give them three hairs from his head to tie his horse to a tree. He did this, and as soon as he had done it, the nymphs blew three times on his three hairs. In a flash, Chiriklo, his horse and his dog changed into three stones.

But far away in Chiriklo's home, Miriklo saw blood on his sabre. He realized that his brother was in some kind of trouble. He mounted his horse, called his dog, attached his sabre, and left his home to find and help his brother.

He followed the same route Chiriklo had taken and he, too, came to the Pasha's city, because he had also become thirsty. He saw the same wise old woman that Chiriklo had met, sitting in the same place. She knew the magic of the two brothers, two horses, two dogs and two sabres and she told him that his brother had been turned into a stone by three nymphs, pointing to the mountain. Then she told him about how his brother had slain the dragons and married the Pasha's rescued daughter.

She advised Miriklo that, if he wanted to help his brother, he should not give anything that belonged to him to the nymphs. Armed with this advice, Miriklo went into the mountain. He found the three nymphs sitting around the fire, surrounded by stones. They asked him for three hairs off his head to tie his horse to a tree, but he told them that he had a chain to do this. Then he sat among them. He began to tell them such funny stories that they could not stop laughing. When they were delirious from laughter, he pushed them into the fire.

At that moment, the effects of their magic disappeared. The stones that had been scattered around the fire started to change, some of them into animals, and many of them into human beings. And, close to him, he recognized his brother and his brother's animals. Chiriklo was coughing, his horse was neighing and his dog was barking. The two brothers hugged each other in relief.

Soon, a beautiful girl walked towards them; and they recognized Terni, Pasha's first daughter. At first sight, Miriklo and she fell in love. They all went back to the Pasha's palace.

The Pasha and Sumnali couldn't believe what they saw: Terni was returned, alive and well! Sumnali was so happy to see her sister alive, after so long.

The Pasha gave permission for Miriklo to claim Terni's hand, and they were soon married.

Chiriklo stayed in the Pasha's city with Sumnali and was given the city as a wedding present by the Pasha. Miriklo went home with Terni because his mother, Queen Papusha, could not stay too long alone.

Sovimahchi Djiljori

Chutem kuna tala e pruna,
Si ma chavo te dav kuna,
Brshind del thaj najarel leh,
Patra peren, ucharen leh,
Buzni nakhel, chuchi del leh,
Bahval phurdel, sovljarel leh.

Purani djili

Lullaby

I will put a cradle under a plum tree,
I will lull my child to sleep;
When it rains, the rain will bathe him,
When the leaves fall, they will hide him,
When a goat passes, it will feed him,
When the wind blows, it will calm him.

Traditional

HEDINA TAHIROVIĆ SIJERČIĆ bijandili 11. 11. 1960. ando Saraj (Sarajevo), Bosna thaj Hercegovina. Voj si sikadi zhurnalisti thaj sikamni. Hedina sasa angluni editori pala Rromane programe pe Radio-Televizijate Sarajevo, thaj angluni Rromni savi gatisarda univerziteto ande Bosna thaj Hercegovina.

Hedina cherda buchi ande Toronto sar regularni sikamni pe Engliski chib pala skolaki themeski organizacija savi akhardol "Toronto District School Board". Voj sasa angluni editori pala angluno Rromano lil ande Kanada pe akhardipe "Romano Lil", 1998-2001.

Hedina akana dzuvdel ande Germanija.

Hedina Sijerčić romasarda :

2009.
- Bosnaki – Rromani alavari, Bosnako alav, Bosna thaj Hercegovina
- Rromani – Bosnaki alavari, Bosnako alav, Bosna thaj Hercegovina
- Jekh bendjali familija (pala chavore) ande Englecki thaj Rromani, Magoria Books Toronto, Kanada
- Sar o Devel cherda e Rromen (pala chavore) ande Englecki, Rromani, Ungaricki, Bosnaki thaj Germanski chib, Magoria Books Toronto, Kanada
- Rromano princo Penga (pala chavore) ande Englecki thaj Rromani, Magoria Books Toronto, Kanada
- Rromane Paramicha (pala pherdebrshenge), ande Englecki thaj Rromani, Magoria Books Toronto, Kanada

2008.
- Tradipe "Ciknoro princo" kataro Bosnaki ande Rromani chib, Bosnako alav, Bosna thaj Hercegovina
- "Stare romske bajke i priče" (Purane Rromane paramicha) ande Bosnaki thaj Rromani chib, Bosnako alav, Bosna thaj Hercegovina

- "Dukh-Pain", ande Rromani thaj Englecki chib, Magoria Books, Kanada
- Tradipe, drama "Hasanaginca", kataro Bosnaki ande Rromani, Bosnako alav, Bosna thaj Hercegovina
- Tradipe, paramichi "Parno them, kotorvalo them", kataro Bosnaki ande Rromani chib, Bosnako alav, Bosna thaj Hercegovina

2004.
- Autorka "Romane Paramicha", ande Englecki thaj Germanski chib, Turnshare, London, Bari Britanija

2001.
- Tradipe "Na dzanen aver, gova si amaro dzuvdipe", kataro Bosnaki ande Rromani chib, Medica Zenica-Infoteka, Bosna thaj Hercegovina

1999.
- Editorka, "Kanadake Romane Mirikle", ande Englecki thaj Rromani chib, Roma Community and Advocacy Centre, Toronto, Kanada

1995.
- Tradipe, "Ilmihal" kataro Serbsko-Hrvatski ande Rromani chib, El-Kalem, Sarajevo, Bosna thaj Hercegovina

1991.
- Tradipe, pala filmo "Ratvali Bijav" kataro Rromani ande Serbsko-Hrvatski chib, TV-Sarajevo, Bosna thaj Hercegovina

1989.
- Dokumentarno TV-filmo "Adjive Romen", TV Sarajevo, Bosna thaj Hercegovina Dokumentarno TV-filmo "Karankochi-Kochi", TV Sarajevo 1989, Bosna thaj Hercegovina

HEDINA TAHIROVIĆ SIJERČIĆ was born on November 11th of 1960 in Sarajevo, Bosnia and Herzegovina. She is a graduate journalist and teacher. She organized and hosted Romani programs for the Radio-TV station in Sarajevo and she was the first of those declared Roma who finished university in Bosnia and Herzegovina.

She later lived in Toronto and worked as a teacher for the Toronto District School Board. While living in Canada she was the Editor-in-Chief of the first Canadian-Romani newsletter, *Romano Lil* from 1998 to 2001.

Presently she is living in Germany.

Published works by Hedina Tahirović Sijerčić include:

2009.

- *Author,* BOSNAKI – ROMANI ALAVARI (BOSNIAN – ROMANI DICTIONARY)

- *Author,* ROMANI – BOSNAKI ALAVARI (ROMANI – BOSNIAN DICTIONARY)

- *Author,* AN UNUSUAL FAMILY (children's book) in English and Romani.
  Magoria Books – Toronto, Canada

- *Author,* HOW GOD MADE THE ROMA (children's book) in English, Romani, Hungarian and German.
  Magoria Books – Toronto, Canada

- *Author,* ROMANI PRINCE PENGA (children's book) in English and Romani.
  Magoria Books – Toronto, Canada

- *Author,* RROMANE PARAMICHA: STORIES AND LEGENDS OF THE GURBETI ROMA in English and Romani.
  Magoria Books – Toronto, Canada

2008.
- *Translator (from Bosnian to Romani),* THE LITTLE PRINCE.
  The Bosnian Word — Bosnia and Herzegovina

104

- *Author*, STARE ROMSKE BAJKE I PRIČE (OLD ROMANI LEGENDS AND FOLKTALES) in Bosnian and Romani.
  The Bosnian Word — Bosnia and Herzegovina
- *Author*, DUKH — PAIN (poetry book) in English and Romani.
  Magoria Books — Toronto, Canada
- *Translator (from Bosnian to Romani)*, HASANAGINCA (play).
  The Bosnian Word — Bosnia and Herzegovina
- *Translator (from Bosnian to Romani)*, WHITE WORLD, COLOURFUL WORLD (folktale).
  The Bosnian Word — Bosnia and Herzegovina

2004.
- *Author*, ROMANY LEGENDS in English and German.
  Turnshare — London, United Kingdom

2001.
- *Translator (from Bosnian to Romani)*, NA DZANEN AVER, GOVA SI AMARO DZUVDIPE (HOW WE LIVE).
  Medica Zenica-Infoteka — Bosnia and Herzegovina

1999.
- *Editor-in-Chief*, CANADIAN ROMANI PEARLS (KANADAKE ROMANE MIRIKLE), in English and Romani.
  Roma Community and Advocacy Centre — Toronto, Canada

1995.
- *Translator (from Serbo-Croatian to Romani)*, ILMIHAL.
  El-Kalem — Sarajevo, Bosnia and Herzegovina

1991.
- *Translator (from Romani to Serbo-Croatian)*, RATVALI BIJAV (BLOOD WEDDING) (feature film).
  TV Sarajevo — Bosnia and Herzegovina

1989.
- ROMA TODAY and KARANKOCHI-KOCHI (documentary films).
  TV Sarajevo — Bosnia and Herzegovina

Also from

MAGORIA BOOKS

DUKH — PAIN

BY HEDINA SIJERČIĆ

Hedina Sijerčić's collection of richly evocative poems weave together the author's fleeting joys and enduring tragedies with traditional Romani folk-lore.

Hedina's poetry is enlightening in its candidness, which shatters the fanciful myth of the mysterious and ever-carefree Roma, replacing it with lyric images of a people living, loving, and dying, not immune to the caprice of the world that surrounds them. It is through such tragedies that the lingering message of these poems has become simply dukh, pain.

MAGORIA BOOKS
www.MagoriaBooks.com

E ZHIVINDI YAG
THE LIVING FIRE

BY RONALD LEE

Ronald Lee's autobiographical novel, formerly published as "Goddam Gypsy", is an intense, fast moving, and brutally honest affair.

Yanko—a Canadian Rom who 'took the non-Romani way but didn't go far'—seeks his fortunes both among and apart from the Roma, never quite finding his place. His story exposes the out of sight, out of mind world of Canada's Roma in 1970's Montréal: Parties, rackets, bar brawls, weddings, desperate poverty, and intermittent police raids fuel in Yanko the passion, creativity, and rebellious defiance that is The Living Fire.

MAGORIA BOOKS
www.MagoriaBooks.com

ROMANI DICTIONARY
(Kalderash - English / English - Kalderash)

BY RONALD LEE

Ronald Lee—internationally renowned author, Romani activist, and Sessional Instructor of the University of Toronto's "The Romani Diaspora" course—brings us the most detailed and accurate Romani–English and English–Romani dictionary set ever to be published.

Intended to be a tool for both native speakers and language learners, the dictionaries provide both grammatical classification and examples through real world phrases, making them the ideal companion volumes to the author's earlier "Learn Romani" and to Ian Hancock's "Handbook of Vlax Romani".

HOW LONG IS THE JOURNEY?
(Photography Book)

BY ZSUZSANNA ARDÓ

Magoria Books is proud to bring you Zsuzsanna Ardó's subtle yet communicative photographs of Hungarian Roma living by the river Danube.

Captioned in English, Hungarian, and Romani, the photographer's pictures bring us a myriad candid moments filled with the extraordinary beauty hidden in quotidian Romani life. The exhibition of the same name, from which this book is sourced, was one of several events chosen by the European Commission to mark the European Year of Intercultural Dialogue (2008), and received praise from as far away as India.

MAGORIA BOOKS
www.MagoriaBooks.com

ROMANI DICTIONARY
(Gurbeti - English / English - Gurbeti)

BY HEDINA SIJERČIĆ

The first comprehensive bi-directional dictionary of the compiler's native Gurbeti Romani dialect, with both grammatical classification and many examples of real-world usage. Ideal for both practical use by native speakers and language learners, as well as for academics interested in lexical comparisons of Romani dialects.

Spoken by large groups of Roma still living in the successor states of the former Yugoslavia, as well as the widely emigrated diaspora created by the turbulent history of the region; Gurbeti Romani is the native language of many a Romani artist and writer, and thus the dialect used in several notable books, Hedina Sijerčić's other titles among them.

ME NI DŽANAV TE KAMAV
(tentative title)

BY RUŽDIJA SEJDOVIĆ

Ruždija Sejdović's intimate and symbolically charged love poems bring into keen focus the passion and suffering of both the poet and his people. The delicately crafted verses shift imperceptably from speaking with the voice of one man to echoing the cries of a rising Romani nation still haunted by European demons.

Containing the author's poems in English and Hungarian in addition to the original Romani; this book aims to be a mirror for and a bridge between peoples both kindred and other.

MAGORIA BOOKS
www.MagoriaBooks.com

About Magoria Books

Magoria Books is an independent international publisher specializing in Romani books. Our aim is to provide Romani authors with opportunities to continue to develop and enrich the ever-growing body of Romani literature.

We would therefore like to encourage Romani poets, writers, and activists to approach us with their ideas and proposals. We are particularly interested in folktales, poetry, and other Romani-focused manuscripts, including those written in the Romani language; but are open to considering other relevant materials.

We are also interested in partnerships with translators, community organizations, and foreign publishers to find ways to increase distribution, availability, and impact of existing and upcoming titles.

Write to us at:

Magoria Books
1562 Danforth Avenue #92006
Toronto, ON M4J 5C1
Canada